Restructuring Rural Saskatchewan

The Challenge of the 1990s

Restructuring Rural Saskatchewan

The Challenge of the 1990s

by

Jack C. Stabler
M.R. Olfert

Canadian Plains Research Center
University of Regina
1992

Canadian Plains Research Center
University of Regina
Regina, Saskatchewan S4S 0A2
Canada

∞

Printed on acid-free paper

Canadian Cataloguing in Publication Data

Stabler, J.C., 1935-

Restructuring rural Saskatchewan: the challenge of the 1990s

    (Canadian plains reports, ISSN 0384-8930 ; no. 9)
    ISBN 0-88977-071-9

1. Cities and towns – Saskatchewan. 2. Rural development – Saskatchewan. 3. Saskatchewan – Economic conditions – 1945- * I. Olfert, M.R. (Margaret Rose), 1950- II. University of Regina. Canadian Plains Research Center. III. Title. IV. Series.

HC117.S2S72 1992   330.97124   C92-098096-1

75051

Cover Design: Agnes Bray, Brian Mlazgar
Printed and bound in Canada by Hignell Printing, Winnipeg, Manitoba

Contents

Figures   vii
Tables   vii
Summary   ix
Acknowledgements   xii

1. Introduction   1
    The Context   1
    Factors Affecting Rural Change   2
    Selective Review of Related Literature   4
    Outline of This Report   7
2. Central Place Theory   8
3. Data Sources and Methodology   12
    Data Sources   12
    Methodology   14
4. Overview of Changes in the Provincial Trade-Centre System:
    1961-1990   16
    Introduction   16
    Changes in the Trade-Centre System: 1961-1990   16
5. Trade-Centre Change by Major Agricultural Regions   23
    Agricultural Areas in Saskatchewan   23
    Community Change by Agricultural Area   26
    Other Factors Affecting Community Viability   34
6. Shopping Patterns and Market Areas   38
    Introduction   38
    Overview of 1991 Shopping Patterns   38
    Detailed Analysis of 1991 Shopping Patterns   40
        Minimum Convenience Centres   40
        Full Convenience Centres   45
        Partial Shopping Centres   47
        Complete Shopping Centres   48
        Wholesale-Retail Centres   48
    A Qualifying Note   50
    Market Areas   50
7. Variations from the General Pattern   53
    Introduction   53
    Proximity to a Major Centre: The Bedroom Effect   53
        1961 Minimum Convenience Cluster   59
        1990 Minimum Convenience Cluster   60

1961 Full Convenience Cluster	60
1990 Full Convenience Cluster	61
Mining Communities	62
Manufacturing Communities	65
8. Public and Private Investment	77
Background	77
Analysis of Expenditures on Infrastructure	78
Investment in Commercial Infrastructure	81
9. Options for the Future	83
References	86

Figures

1. Agricultural Economic Areas in Saskatchewan   25
2. Selected Characteristics of Minimum Convenience Centres:
   Southern Relative to Northern   27
3. Selected Characteristics of Full Convenience Centres:
   Southern Relative to Northern   27
4. Selected Characteristics of Partial Shopping Centres:
   Southern Relative to Northern   28
5. Selected Characteristics of Complete Shopping Centres:
   Southern Relative to Northern   28
6. Shopping Patterns of Rural Residents by Proximity
   of Residence to Class of Trade Centre   39

Tables

1. n-Orders of Functions Provided by m-Levels of Centres   9
2. Summary Description of Saskatchewan Trade-Centre System:
   1961, 1981, and 1990   17
3. Age Distribution by Functional Classification, Saskatchewan
   Trade Centres: 1990   19
4. Average Number of Businesses of Various Types in
   Saskatchewan Trade Centres: 1990   20
5. Saskatchewan Communities in Top Four Functional
   Categories: 1990   21
6. Saskatchewan Farm Size by Agricultural Area: 1961-1986   24
7. Difference Profile: 1961   30
8. Difference Profile: 1981   31
9. Difference Profile: 1990   32
10. Proportion of Communities Declining, Remaining Stable,
    or Growing by Period   33
11. Number and Percent of High-Level Centres in Each
    Economic Area: 1961, 1981, and 1990   34
12. Population Change by Agricultural Areas: 1961-1990   36
13. Shopping Patterns of Rural Residents Living Near
    Minimum Convenience Centres: 1991   41
14. Shopping Patterns of Rural Residents Living Near
    Minimum Convenience Centres: 1991   42
15. Shopping Patterns of Rural Residents Living Near
    Minimum Convenience Centres: 1991   43

16. Shopping Patterns of Rural Residents Living Near
    Full Convenience Centres: 1991   46
17. Shopping Patterns of Rural Residents Living Near
    Partial Shopping Centres: 1991   47
18. Shopping Patterns of Rural Residents Living Near
    Complete Shopping Centres: 1991   49
19. Distances Travelled by Rural Dwellers to Shop by
    Functional Classification of Centre   51
20. Residuals Comparing 1961 Minimum Convenience
    Bedroom Communities with the Non-Bedroom Communities
    in Minimum Convenience Category in 1961   56
21. Residuals Comparing 1961 Full Convenience Bedroom
    Communities with the Non-Bedroom Communities in
    Full Convenience Category in 1961   57
22. Communities Adjacent to Mines   62
23. Difference Profiles Comparing Remote Mining
    Communities with Other Remote Communities by
    Initial Functional Classification   64
24. Difference Profile for Secondary Wholesale-Retail
    Communities (Means of the Northern Zone Minus Means
    of the Southern Zone)   66
25. Difference Profile for Secondary Wholesale-Retail
    Communities (Means of the Northern Zone Minus Means
    of the Transition Zone)   67
26. Difference Profile for Primary Wholesale-Retail
    Communities (Means of the Northern Zone Minus Means
    of the Transition Zone)   69
27. Communities in the Lower Four Functional Categories
    With More than Forty Manufacturing Employees in 1990   71
28. Difference Profile for Complete Shopping Centres
    (Communities with Manufacturing Employment > 100 -
    All Other Complete Shopping Centres)   72
29. Difference Profile for Partial Shopping Centres (Communities
    with Manufacturing Employment > 40 < 100 - All Other
    Partial Shopping Centres)   73
30. Population and Provincial Government Plus SWP Investment   79
31. Cumulative Expenditures on Community Infrastructure
    by Functional Classification   80

Summary

This report is the second of two focussing on changes in the system of communities that constitute Saskatchewan's trade-centre hierarchy. The first, entitled *The Changing Role of Rural Communities in an Urbanizing World: Saskatchewan 1961-1990*, was published earlier this year by the Canadian Plains Research Center, University of Regina.

Both studies employ central place theory as a theoretical context for analysis. Within this framework, communities are grouped into six functional categories. In order of increasing specialization these are: Minimum Convenience, Full Convenience, Partial Shopping, Complete Shopping, Secondary Wholesale-Retail, and Primary Wholesale-Retail centres.

The initial study, conducted at a relatively macrolevel, identified the structure of the system at three points in time: 1961, 1981, and 1990. A great deal of attention was devoted to analyzing changes in the structure of the hierarchy between these dates. In general, the top three functional levels gained population and business outlets between 1961 and 1981 and between 1981 and 1990 at the expense of the lower three levels. Even so, concentration at the top of the system increased as the number of communities in the three highest functional categories decreased from thirty-nine in 1961 to thirty-two in 1981 and sixteen in 1990.

A geographical division of the province into three agricultural zones proved very useful in interpreting changes within functional categories. A lower rate of decline from one functional classification to the next characterized communities in the more diversified northern agricultural zone compared with those in the southern and transition zones.

While the initial study focussed on changes to the structure of the system, this report takes the analysis to a finer level of detail and concentrates on changes that have affected particular types of communities and smaller geographic areas.

A more in-depth comparison of communities among the three

agricultural zones is followed by an analysis of the geographic extent of the bedroom effect around the province's major cities.

Shopping patterns, which have both a geographic and a functional influence on the viability of individual communities as well as the structure of the system, are investigated for thirty-one goods and services ranging from very common to very complex items.

At an even finer level, the contribution to a community's viability of a mine or a manufacturing activity located in close proximity is investigated.

Finally, the pattern of infrastructure investment during the 1980s is analyzed.

In general these microanalyses have identified one set of influences which, on balance, is contributing to the consolidation of the system and another set which is tending to oppose consolidation.

Changes in production, transportation, communications and distribution technology have either led to reduced labour requirements or to centralization for other reasons. The net effect has been a loss of rural activity relative to that in urban areas. Shopping patterns and infrastructure investment, too, have a strong centralizing influence that extends all across the province.

Diversification within agriculture, on the other hand, appears to have contributed to diversification in other sectors of the economy in the northern zone and this has slowed the process of consolidation somewhat in that area. For individual communities, or perhaps the community and its immediately surrounding area, the presence of a major mine or several manufacturing firms contributes to the stabilization of the community's population. In the case of well-located centres, already performing a locally important role in the trade- centre system, such activities can stabilize or possibly even strengthen the community's trade-centre function as well. The growth of the major cities has led to consolidation on a macroscale through capturing a substantial portion of the trade once conducted in smaller centres. At the same time, this same growth has led to decentralization on a microscale as small communities close to the largest centres have become rural suburbs of the larger places. On balance, centralizing influences have been much stronger than those offsetting consolidation. This experience is not unique to Saskatchewan.

Rural economies across all of North America have been going through a process of structural adjustment for several decades. Prior to the 1980s these adjustments occurred in a context of generally higher commodity prices, buoyant nonrural labour markets and a technological lead over much of the rest of the world which generated surpluses that could be used to soften the adjustment process.

During most of the 1980s commodity prices have been low, the technology gap has been closed, and urban labour markets have been slack. Difficulties experienced by rural economies during the past decade have become well known. It does not appear that the economic environment within which rural restructuring must continue will revert to that which characterized the 1970s. Global markets, the failure of GATT to restore order to international markets for agricultural products, loss of technological leadership across many industries, the emergence of trade blocs within which competition will be vigorous and between which barriers will continue to exist, all imply that future structural adjustment will occur in a much more Spartan environment than that which characterized much of North America's economic history.

The challenge facing the people of Saskatchewan at this time is to acknowledge that past efforts to prevent the adjustment have failed, that continued restructuring is inevitable, and that future adjustments will occur in an austere economic environment. Within this context an approach must be chosen that will guide efforts to restructure the rural economy so that it can effectively participate in the economic and social order of the 1990s and beyond.

Acknowledgements

Funding for the research that made this report possible was provided by several agencies which we are pleased to acknowledge. In alphabetic order these agencies were:

Agriculture Canada: Policy Branch, Ottawa
College of Agriculture: University of Saskatchewan, Saskatoon
Credit Union Central of Saskatchewan: Regina
Department of Diversification and Economic Development,
    Government of Saskatchewan, Regina

The authors would like to thank Agnes Bray and Brian Mlazgar of the Canadian Plains Research Center, University of Regina, for their work in preparing this book for publication. Capable research assistance was provided by Jocelyn Hamoline, Darren Filson, Michelle Stabler, Mitch Wensley, and Jacynthe Wionzek.

1

Introduction

The Context

While the 1970s are now remembered as the decade of "rural renaissance," the 1980s have come to be classified as the decade of rural decline. Increasingly, during the past several years, a growing awareness has developed in every segment of society that all is not well in rural North America.

Agriculture is one of the basic industries on this continent and several subsectors of this industry have been under stress for most of the 1980s.

Saskatchewan has one of the highest concentrations of employment in agriculture of any political subdivision in North America. Continentwide, less than 5 percent of the labour force is engaged in agriculture while, for Saskatchewan, the corresponding figure is approximately 18 percent.

Saskatchewan is also more rural than most other political subdivisions. There are no cities in Saskatchewan with more than 200,000 population. Further, 50 percent of Saskatchewan's population lives either in rural areas or in communities with fewer than 10,000 residents. For Canada as a whole, 59 percent of the nation's population lives in urban concentrations exceeding 200,000 while only 30 percent of the population lives in rural areas or communities smaller than 10,000.

Macrostatistics which reflect economic and social well-being reveal a worsening of rural conditions, compared with the same indicators for urban areas. For example, rural population size across North America was stagnant or declined during the 1980s while urban population size increased. Rural unemployment rates were above those for urban areas and rose relative to urban unemployment rates during the past decade. Poverty rates as well were higher in rural areas and rose relative to urban poverty during the 1980s (USDA, 1990, 1991; Bollman, 1990).

1

A portion of the general population appears to attribute the unfavourable conditions in rural areas today to the low agricultural commodity prices which characterized most of the 1980s. This is a misinterpretation. Low commodity prices have exacerbated the situation during much of the 1980s; but commodity prices are not the sole, nor even the major, cause of today's rural problems as a few facts will illustrate.

Other rural areas, whose economic base is in some activity other than agriculture, have also declined during the 1980s. Across North America, rural economies based on manufacturing, retirement or mining have declined along with those which, like Saskatchewan, are based primarily on agriculture. Further, a review of the statistics for previous decades reveals that rural-based activity, generally, contracted during the 1940s, 1950s, and 1960s as well as during the 1980s (Hathaway, 1960; Reed, 1989; Barkley, 1990). For some rural economies, the 1970s was a period of expansion. For Saskatchewan, this was not the case. While farm incomes, and incomes generated in some other extractive industries, were high in Saskatchewan during the 1970s, on balance Saskatchewan's rural economy contracted even during the 1970s (Stabler, 1987a).

As these few facts illustrate, Saskatchewan's experience is not unique. Rural economies across North America, with a variety of economic bases, have been under considerable stress during the 1980s. For many rural areas this decline represents a return to a long-term trend going back many decades.

Factors Affecting Rural Change

A closer examination reveals a number of influences, many of long standing, which have led to the unfavourable circumstances which characterize rural Saskatchewan, and much of rural North America, today. Such a review reveals that many of the negative impacts on rural areas were unintended consequences of the adoption or acceptance of changes that were necessary or beneficial when considered on their own merits.

One influence, going back many decades, has been the substitution of capital for labour in agriculture. While increasing productivity per person, mechanization also resulted in consolidation of farm holdings and the outmigration of farm families from rural areas (Furtan and Lee, 1977; Barkley, 1990).

Another powerful and long-standing influence has been the change in shopping patterns of rural dwellers occasioned by both the urbanization of rural tastes and improvements in the transportation system. Once content to shop in nearby communities which provided convenience at the expense of variety and competitive prices, rural dwellers have extended the range they are prepared to travel to obtain additional choice and lower prices. Small communities were bypassed in the process and subsequently lost trade and service outlets, while cities and regional shopping centres expanded and prospered (Stabler and Williams, 1973; Stabler, 1987a; Anding et al., 1990).

In the public sector, as well, a substantial amount of consolidation has occurred. Over 2,700 schools in rural areas and small towns in Saskatchewan were closed between 1951 and 1971 as students were bussed into elementary schools in nearby communities or to regionally central high schools. During the 1960s and 1970s, 390 rural post offices were closed (Stabler, 1987a). And, as population has moved from the country to the town and to the city, expenditures on infrastructure have shifted as well. Thus the infrastructure of growing towns and cities is continuously expanded and upgraded while that in smaller communities and rural areas deteriorates and is downgraded or removed. Further, infrastructure embodying new technologies such as fibre optics or hazardous waste disposal are seldom built in rural areas.

Both the change in shopping patterns and the consolidation of school systems mentioned above were facilitated by yet another improvement — the upgrading of the intercity highway network. Between 1951 and 1971 paved highways in Saskatchewan increased from 750 to 10,000 miles and several thousand additional miles have been paved since.

More recently, and less directly, changes occurring in the structure of the North American economy have had an adverse effect on rural economies. One of these is the shift from a product-producing to a services-dominant industrial structure. During the period following World War II the improved infrastructure in rural areas — paved roads, power, water and sewage systems — led to an expansion of routine manufacturing activity which provided jobs for some of those leaving agriculture. With the subsequent automation of manufacturing processes, which downgraded the skills required, and the lowering of barriers to international trade, many routine manufacturing operations have moved offshore. At the economywide level, the growth of the service sector has replaced these jobs numerically but has not replaced the lost income because of lower wages in the service industries. Further, the high skill-high technology service jobs are almost exclusively an urban-based phenomenon. Service-sector jobs created in rural areas have been concentrated in low-skill, part-time, and low-pay activities (John, Batie and Norris, 1989; Reed, 1989).

Finally, even the macroeconomic policies used by governments to manage the national economy have had a differential adverse effect on rural areas. The high interest rates employed to control inflation during much of the past fifteen years have inhibited investment in capital-intensive facilities required for the extractive and primary-production processes which characterize rural industry.

Selective Review of Related Literature

A very large literature, developed within the context of central place theory, has emerged over the past four decades primarily through the efforts of regional scientists, geographers and regional economists. Much of this literature is theoretical and deals with alternative functional or spatial arrangements and how changes in some of the critical variables affect the equilibrium state of the model. The present study of structural adjustment in Saskatchewan was definitely guided by this body of received theory. An interesting recent summary is found in Mulligan (1984). A useful summary of contributions to both the theoretical and empirical literature focussing on market centres and the location of retail outlets is found in Berry et al. (1988). Each summary includes a wealth of references back to the 1950s.

Comprehensive empirical studies of complete trade-centre systems are rare. Those comparing complete systems at two or more points in time are even more scarce. Two reports included in the first category, which have some bearing on the prairie situation, are Borchert and Adams's impressive study of trade centres in the upper midwest (1963) and Hodge's study of Saskatchewan (1965). In the latter category are studies by Stabler (1987a) for Saskatchewan between 1961 and 1981 and Anding et al. (1990) who updated the Borchert and Adams's study and catalogued changes in the trade-centre system of the upper midwest between 1960 and 1989. A recent study of trade-centre change in North Dakota between 1970 and 1988 by Bangsund et al. (1991) identifies numerous structural adjustments similar to those observed for Saskatchewan in the present study.

Another line of inquiry, developed (almost) independently of the central-place literature just referenced, has focussed on relationships between rural communities and their agricultural hinterlands. This literature, a product of research conducted mainly by rural sociologists and agricultural economists, goes back to the 1930s. Recent summaries, with voluminous historical references, can be found in Nuckton et al. (1982), Swanson (1988) and Luloff and Swanson (1990).

Empirical analyses, conducted either within the rural communities or the central-place framework, have generally employed a macro approach. Central-place studies have typically described a system's structure at a point in time or identified changes occurring through time. Little effort has been put toward empirically searching for explanations of the changes noted. Studies conducted in the rural-communities context have identified associations between community characteristics and a range of agricultural variables but, again, little effort has been focussed on attempting to precisely establish cause and effect relationships.

A few exceptions to this generalization should be noted. John et al. (1988) compared employment growth in 548 rural counties in the central-midwestern United States between 1979 and 1984 in an effort to determine whether there were any rural economies in which local initiatives had produced positive results. In the end only eight counties emerged as candidates. To this list were added an additional eight on the advice of local officials. A variety of approaches in these counties had produced "success" built around several different types of economic activity. Their study has little to say about the types of communities that could reasonably expect to become centres for rural growth but does offer insights that could be useful to provincial and local governments attempting to organize a development initiative.

A second study by Carlino and Mills (1987) explored the determinants of population and employment densities in 3,000 United States counties during the 1970s. While macro in approach, this work did investigate the relationships between employment and population growth and exogenous variables describing local economic conditions. Since rural economies had such a dramatically different experience during the 1980s than during the period analyzed, however, it is the approach that is interesting rather than the empirical results.

Some older studies are also of interest, more for the techniques utilized than their findings. Among these is one by Levine and Adelman (1973) who used factor analysis to analyze the variance in income growth in 578 counties in Appalachia. Finally, Barnard, MacMillan, and Maki (1969) used a two-region input-output model to study the effectiveness of a federal-provincial regional development program in the Interlake area of Manitoba in the 1960s.

There are numerous papers on policy, some derived primarily from theory and others based on empirical analyses, conducted within a variety of theoretical constructs. The most comprehensive review of this literature, to the time of its publication, is contained in Jansma (1982). Several other older works which have sufficient generality to warrant specific mention include Nevin (1966), Jansma and Goode (1976), Edwards (1976), and Redman (1980).

In the late 1980s and early 1990s several books and articles on rural-development policy have appeared. Many describe the current state of distress in rural areas as a prelude to policy prescription but virtually none have benefitted from the detailed empirical analysis required to identify with precision not only how, but also why, rural economies are depressed, and how the rural environment of the 1990s differs from that in any previous period. Such analyses have massive data requirements and the numbers on which such investigations rely are just becoming available. Recent works on policy include books by Brown et al. (1988), Luloff and Swanson (1990), Pigg (1991), and Flora and Christenson (1991). Each contains a substantial bibliography.

Outline of This Report

This report will chronicle the changes occurring in the system of communities serving rural Saskatchewan. Following brief discussions of theory and methodology, we provide an overview of the changes in the structure of the trade-centre system during the past thirty years. In subsequent sections we focus on particular factors that may have had a greater influence in some areas of the province than others, or on some types of communities than others.

In the first instance we investigate the influence of agricultural diversification on community viability in different areas of the province. Another pervasive influence, capable of stimulating some communities while neglecting others, is associated with the spatial distribution of demand. In our second investigation, we identify the types of communities in which rural dwellers obtain a range of products, some as common as gasoline and others as complex as major surgery.

We then look at the influence of proximity to large urban areas — in particular, the tendency for satellite or bedroom communities to develop around the province's major cities.

Major investments in or near a community, such as mines or manufacturing plants, are thought to contribute to a centre's viability. We investigate both phenomena and attempt to identify the effect that a major mine or a major manufacturing presence has had on those communities where such events have occurred.

Finally, we consider the importance of public expenditures on infrastructure and the relationship between such expenditures and population concentrations in Saskatchewan during the 1980s.

The last section provides conclusions and our interpretations of these findings for the future of the rural economy generally and the trade-centre system particularly.

2

Central Place Theory

Central place theory is the theory most widely used to explain the number, size, and spacing of centres in a system of urban places. According to this theory, the role of the central place is to act as a service and distribution centre for its hinterland, providing its own, and the adjacent population, with goods and services. The reason why such functions are provided from central places is given by the concepts of the demand threshold and the range of the good. The threshold is defined in terms of the minimum level of population and income required to support a particular activity, while the range refers to the maximum area that the activity in question can serve from a particular place. The range is limited because transport costs raise the price of the item as distance from the central place increases. This is true regardless of whether the item is a good distributed from the centre or is one that customers have to travel to the centre to obtain.

Since the threshold and range will differ among various activities, a hierarchical spatial structure results in which the activity with the lowest threshold requirement is found in all central places. In today's context a gasoline station would typify a service function with a low-demand threshold. Only a small population is required to provide the level of demand necessary to support a gasoline station. Consequently, many exist and they are distributed widely — wherever a small concentration of population is found. Activities requiring a larger threshold, however, are found in fewer and larger places. Since the size of service areas vary directly with the size of centres, the complementary regions of small places are contained within those of larger places. Table 1 illustrates how n-orders of functions are provided by m-levels of centres.

The number of functions of each type required, and thus the number of centres of each size within the system, is largely a function of total population and income, while the spacing of centres is determined by population density and accessibility. Higher incomes and larger populations are associated with a greater number of functions. The number of centres is directly related to population density but is inversely related to the quality of the region's transportation systems.

Table 1
n-Orders of Functions Provided by m-Levels of Centres

Order of Function			Level of Centre			
	Lowest	m-4	m-3	m-2	m-1	m
n						x
n-1					x	x
n-2				x	x	x
n-3			x	x	x	x
n-4		x	x	x	x	x
lowest	x	x	x	x	x	x

Referring to Table 1, it is apparent that the lowest level of centre would provide only the lowest-order function. The next largest community, m-4, would also provide the lowest-order function to its own and the immediately adjacent rural population. But the larger community also offers the next highest-order function, n-4. These services are provided to its own residents plus the population contained within several adjacent centres of the lowest order and all of the rural population contained within this larger market area. Each successively higher-order function, offered from increasingly higher-level centres, is provided to all lower-level centres and the rural populations within the ever larger market areas of the higher-order functions. Often several functions will have approximately the same demand threshold and a similar range. Thus the number of functions of any given order will typically be greater than the single function implied in Table 1.

Distortions from the theoretical model occur in response to several common phenomena. Rugged topography or uneven resource distribution, for example, lead to uneven population distribution and to transport networks which provide better access to some areas than others. Further, the theory provides a better explanation of the functioning of centres in agricultural, than in highly industrialized, regions. The service-centre role is more clearly apparent when there are few places of large size in a region. When there are several large centres of similar size there is a greater possibility of specialization by function, such as manufacturing or government for example, which may lead to a distortion of the urban-size hierarchy.

In spite of these qualifications, the theory is the most useful one available for the analysis of trade-centre systems. No other theory stresses so much the fundamental interdependence between the community and the region within which it is located. Further, at the operational level, the theoretical relationships specified are capable of empirical verification.

Central place theory is well suited for the topic at hand. Saskatchewan's economy was initially based on agriculture and this sector still provides the basis for much of the employment and income generated within the province. The majority of Saskatchewan's communities came into existence to serve the needs of the agricultural economy. Indeed, their locations were determined primarily by the transportation requirements of the grain industry. Most Saskatchewan communities still perform an agricultural trade-centre function. In addition, there are no really large cities in the province. The largest, Saskatoon and Regina, have specialized to a limited extent but both still are dominant communities in the province's trade-centre system.

Central place theory describes a system in equilibrium; that is, one in which population size and distribution, income and technology are unchanging. Because of this property it is referred to as a static equilibrium theory. This might at first appear as a drawback because we know that technology, income and consequently the province's total population and its distribution have changed significantly over the past several decades. The apparent limitations of a static theory are circumvented to a degree by performing what is referred to as comparative static analysis. In this form of analysis the characteristics of the system are completely identified at two points in time. In a dynamic economy the system would be expected to differ at dates separated by several years. These differences then become the focus of attention and an effort is made to interpret and explain the changes noted by reference to evolving technologies, improvements in transportation, rising incomes, behaviour of people as both consumers and producers, as well as other influences which may become apparent in the conduct of the analysis.[1]

The study of Saskatchewan's trade-centre system in the following chapters is conducted using central place theory and a comparative static approach.

NOTES

1. A thorough discussion of central place theory is available in Berry et al. (1988).

3

Data Sources and Methodology

Data Sources

Communities included in this analysis were those 598 incorporated and unincorporated places which, in 1961, had fifty or more inhabitants. For this group of communities data were initially collected, and the analysis performed, for 1961 to 1981, in a study completed in the mid-1980s (Stabler, 1987a). The same communities were subsequently included in a study of the 1981-1990 period completed in mid-1991 (Stabler, Olfert and Fulton, 1992). The data used for the two previous studies form the basis for this report which investigates factors affecting community viability at a more detailed level than was possible in the earlier publications.

Data describing each community were collected from a variety of sources. Information on the number of business outlets in the communities were obtained primarily from the Dun and Bradstreet *Reference Book*. The businesses are listed according to individual Standard Industrial Classification (SIC) codes. These SIC codes were grouped into thirty-six categories representing groups of businesses commonly found in prairie centres. The number of businesses in each group were then tabulated for each of the 598 communities for 1961, 1981 and 1990.

Several business functions were not adequately represented in Dun and Bradstreet. Further, data for infrastructure and some professional services are not available from this source. Information on the number of grain elevators, banks, credit unions, other financial institutions, dentists, lawyers, doctors, hospital beds, special care facilities, elementary and high school enrolments, postsecondary educational institutions, and real estate offices were obtained from other sources. Professional associations provided data on the location of their members. Banks and the Saskatchewan Credit Union Central contributed a list of the number of their outlets in each community. Education and health care data originated with provincial government departments. The number of elevators and elevator capacity are described in publications from the Canadian Grain Commission. Community profiles, prepared by the provincial Department of Rural Development, provided supplementary information for some of the communities.

Population data, and age distributions of the populations, were obtained primarily from Saskatchewan Health's *Covered Population* statistics and were in some cases augmented with, or crosschecked against, census records.

Information regarding commuting distances of persons working in, but not residents of, Saskatchewan's largest thirty-one centres was obtained from special tabulations of the 1981 census. Commuting distances were calculated as weighted averages for people working in these thirty-one communities but living outside the centre of their employment.

Shopping patterns, identifying where rural dwellers obtain some thirty-one goods and services, were derived from questionnaires returned by Saskatchewan farm families during the spring of 1991. The goods and services used to define shopping patterns were based on the SIC codes employed in classifying communities into functional classifications.

In addition to the statistical data, formal interviews were conducted in some three dozen rural communities over an eight-month period. Groups ranging in size from four to fourteen people were assembled to represent community leaders, town administrators, economic development officers, rural municipality administrators, and the business community. Preliminary results of the statistical analysis were presented to these groups to obtain their input and impressions of the accuracy and validity of the data describing their community, as well as to provide insights into the interpretation of the data. Several dozen additional communities were visited, without interviews, both as a crosscheck on the statistical profiles and to provide additional, more subjective, interpretation.

All of the tables and figures in this report were derived from these data bases unless otherwise indicated. Sources are not identified on each individual presentation, however, because they are typically too numerous.

Methodology

In order to group the communities in the study into functional categories a cluster analysis program was utilized. Cluster analysis is a classificatory technique designed to select subsets of mutually similar objects from the set of all such objects. In this case the task is to select subsets of functionally similar communities from the entire set of 598 communities. Each community is described by a comprehensive set of attributes, all of which are considered simultaneously in the classification scheme. The relevant quantifiable characteristics of a community include population size (and age distribution), the entire array of business functions, and the additional infrastructure as described under "Data Sources" in the preceding section. Through a complex computer algorithm, the program is able to evaluate, compare, and ultimately group centres on the basis of their similarities in terms of the dimensions in which they are described.

For the cluster analysis, the raw data were standardized prior to clustering in order to facilitate comparison of such disparate variables as population size and number of grocery stores. A similarity matrix was subsequently computed where the coefficients represent the distance between communities. Clusters were formed using Ward's (or Orloci's) method which minimizes the distance between the subject and its group centroid as fusion proceeds. Other methods of clustering were also evaluated.

After the initial formation of clusters, the compactness and distinctness of the clusters were tested. An iterative relocation option was utilized to find local optima and a test of whether these local optima represented global efficiency was performed by reinitiating the iterative relocation procedure from several radically different starting classifications. The local optima were found to be very robust. The validity of the groupings was further tested using a t-test for the significance of the differences in the means of the population size and the number of business outlets of adjacent clusters. Finally, the classifications were evaluated using multiple discriminant analysis. In all cases the groups were found to be statistically valid.

This technique resulted in the formation of six distinct clusters for the 1990 data as well as for the two preceding time periods. Given the theoretical context for the analysis, these six clusters are taken to represent the functional categories in a trade-centre hierarchy as described in chapter 2. These categories are commonly described as Minimum Convenience, Full Convenience, Partial Shopping, Complete Shopping, Secondary Wholesale-Retail, and Primary Wholesale-Retail centres.

In the following chapters we use the data and computer programs just described to identify the way in which the structure of the trade-centre system has changed through time. We also discuss the experience of groups of communities in terms of the importance of the types of economies they serve, their size, location, and functional characteristics, the presence of major employers such as mines or manufacturing firms, and the importance of provincial government expenditures for the creation, maintenance, or upgrading of public infrastructure.

4

Overview of Changes in the
Provincial Trade-Centre System: 1961-1990

Introduction

In this chapter we summarize the changes that have taken place in the structure of the trade-centre system between 1961 and 1990.

Profiles of the system were developed for three points in time — 1961, 1981, and 1990 — using the cluster analysis program discussed in chapter 3. It is important to note that, as the structure of the system changes, individual communities are frequently reclassified; that is, they move from one category, such as Partial Shopping centre, to another, such as Full Convenience centre. Over the three decades covered in this study the experience of most communities was a downward reclassification of one or more levels.

Changes in the Trade-Centre System: 1961-1990

The number of communities in each functional classification and their summary descriptions for 1961, 1981, and 1990 are presented in Table 2. Between 1961 and 1981, a very substantial downward movement of communities from the middle categories occurred. In 1961, for example, there were 317 communities situated in the three clusters between the Secondary Wholesale-Retail level and the lowest functional classification, the Minimum Convenience centre. By 1981, the number occupying this interval had decreased to 188.

Between 1981 and 1990 there was some further downward movement of centres in the middle categories, but at a much slower rate. The number of communities in the three clusters between the Secondary Wholesale-Retail and the Minimum Convenience levels declined from 188 in 1981 to 169 in 1990. What is most striking about the latter period is the pronounced decline of communities that were of Complete Shopping centre status in 1981 — only six centres (27 percent) remained in this category in 1990.

Table 2
Summary Description of Saskatchewan Trade-Centre System:
1961, 1981 and 1990

Averages of Population and Business Outlets ± One Standard Deviation

Functional	No. of Centres			1961		1981		1990	
Classification	1961	1981	1990	Pop.	Bus.	Pop.	Bus.	Pop.	Bus.
				115,582	1,649.2	164,345	3,758.3	183,488	4,508.0
Primary	2	2	2	103,834	1,525.5	158,379	3,438.0	181,444	4,213.5
Wholesale/Retail				92,086	1,401.3	152,413	3,117.7	179,400	3,929.0
				23,661	399.7	27,071	754.1	28,269	764.6
Secondary	8	8	8	14,160	286.8	16,713	543.8	18,088	532.6
Wholesale/Retail				4,659	173.9	6,355	333.5	7,907	350.6
				3,166	99.4	4,148	180.9	5,776	232.5
Complete	29	22	6	2,198	77.7	3,032	133.5	4,872	196.2
Shopping Centre				1,230	56.0	1,916	86.1	3,968	159.9
				923	40.6	1,814	71.6	2,593	95.4
Partial	99	30	46	659	33.0	1,296	56.7	1,759	70.0
Shopping Centre				395	25.4	778	41.8	834	44.6
				418	21.2	786	28.3	869	30.8
Full	189	136	117	296	16.9	541	20.8	575	21.3
Convenience Centre				174	12.6	296	13.3	281	11.8
				181	9.2	237	8.0	287	8.6
Minimum	271	400	419	121	6.3	125	4.6	141	4.1
Convenience Centre				61	3.4	13	1.2	—	—

Throughout the 1961-90 period, Saskatchewan was going through a process of urbanization. The population of the 598 subject communities was 538,666 in 1961 (approximately 58 percent of the province's total). By 1981 there were 679,622 people living in these centres (approximately 70 percent) and by 1990 the population of the 598 communities was 744,092. With the provincial population at about one million at this time, the subject communities were home to approximately 74 percent of Saskatchewan's people.

The distribution of the population gain was quite uneven however. Between 1961 and 1981 there was a pronounced relative shift toward the larger centres. The thirty-two communities in the top three functional categories in 1981 had captured 93 percent of the increase experienced by the 598 centres during the preceding twenty years. In terms of number of business outlets, the shift was even more pronounced. The same thirty-two communities gained over 6,500 businesses between 1961 and 1981 while the remaining 566 lost nearly 1,800. The growth of the two largest cities, Saskatoon and Regina, was very substantial in absolute terms, as shown in Table 2, and in relative terms as well.

Saskatchewan's business cycle is characterized by wide fluctuations because of the variability in prices received for the basic commodities that form the core of the province's export base. Nevertheless, the period between 1961 and 1981 was characterized by substantial gains. There was a net increase of over 100,000 jobs during these twenty years. Total real personal expenditure on goods and services increased by 210 percent between these same dates. During the years following 1981, gains have been much slower. Net employment increased from 425,000 to 449,000 by 1990 (a 6 percent increase) while real personal expenditure increased by only 18 percent.

The pace of urbanization was not very different between the latter and the earlier period, although new businesses were created at only about one-third of the previous rate. Further, the distribution of the gains differed from the earlier period in that they were concentrated in even fewer communities. The sixteen communities in the top three functional classifications in 1990 captured 94 percent of the population increase realized by the entire urban system between 1981 and 1990 (compared with 93 percent by thirty-two communities in the top three groups between 1961 and 1981). The gain in business outlets was also more concentrated. Regina and Saskatoon gained 1,551 businesses. The eight Secondary Wholesale-Retail centres combined lost eighty-nine. The six centres remaining in the Complete Shopping centre classification gained 133. The remaining 582 communities lost 832 businesses.

The age structure of the population living in Saskatchewan's communities reflects the economic fortunes of the different categories of trade centres. As shown in Table 3, Saskatoon and Regina especially, but the top three categories of trade centres generally, have a higher proportion of their populations in the labour-

Table 3
Age Distribution by Functional Classification,
Saskatchewan Trade Centres: 1990

Functional Classification	Age Group				
	0-19 (%)	20-44 (%)	45-64 (%)	65+ (%)	Total
Minimum Convenience Centre	14,809 (29)	16,819 (33)	9,023 (18)	10,469 (20)	51,120
Full Convenience Centre	18,378 (27)	20,879 (31)	11,663 (17)	16,194 (24)	67,114
Partial Shopping Centre	21,580 (27)	25,531 (32)	14,657 (18)	19,133 (24)	80,901
Complete Shopping Centre	8,707 (30)	10,625 (36)	4,744 (16)	5,158 (18)	29,234
Secondary Wholesale-Retail	42,783 (30)	55,490 (38)	24,761 (17)	21,672 (15)	144,706
Primary Wholesale-Retail	105,123 (29)	161,503 (45)	59,701 (16)	36,560 (10)	362,887
Total	211,380 (28.7)	290,847 (39.5)	124,549 (16.9)	109,186 (14.8)	735,962

force age groups (roughly ages twenty to sixty-four). Consequently they have lower dependency ratios, that is people under twenty and over sixty-five relative to those in the working-age groups. The choice of retirement centres is also reflected in this population profile. The largest absolute number of people of retirement age, sixty-five and over, live in the province's ten cities. But the highest relative concentrations of people in the sixty-five and over age group are found in the Full Convenience and Partial Shopping centres. It is noteworthy that the percentage of people sixty-five and over living in the smallest class of centres is significantly lower than in the next two larger categories. It seems likely that the avoidance of Minimum Convenience centres may be due to the virtual absence of health care facilities in the 419 communities in this category.

To summarize the comparison between the earlier and latter periods, urbanization continued at roughly the same pace but provincial economic growth was much slower over the decade of the 1980s than during the previous two decades. Slower provincial growth was accompanied by a much slower pace in the creation of

Table 4
Average Number of Businesses of Various Types
in Saskatchewan Trade Centres: 1990

Type of Business	419 Minimum Convenience	117 Full Convenience	46 Partial Shopping	6 Complete Shopping	8 Secondary Wholesale/ Retail	2 Primary Wholesale/ Retail
All Consumers' Serv	2.41	12.42	44.00	123.83	309.25	2057.50
General Store	0.33	0.96	2.50	3.33	5.00	19.50
Grocery Store	0.25	1.20	3.70	6.67	16.50	72.50
Special Food	—	0.37	1.59	4.17	8.25	55.50
Auto Sales	—	0.35	1.80	4.17	10.88	46.50
Gas Station	0.29	1.39	3.57	6.83	19.13	99.00
Clothing Store	—	0.56	3.50	13.33	20.63	147.00
Furniture Store	—	—	0.87	2.50	5.38	42.00
Home Furnishing	—	0.23	1.89	7.50	23.25	142.00
Restaurant	0.16	1.16	3.65	13.00	42.25	342.50
Drug Store	—	0.42	1.52	2.67	6.63	34.50
Special Retail	—	0.44	3.46	12.33	36.75	246.00
Credit Agency	0.27	1.32	3.96	16.17	39.88	388.00
Hotel	0.47	1.40	3.72	8.17	15.88	51.00
Laundries	—	—	0.28	0.83	2.25	22.00
Personal Serv	—	—	0.78	2.33	6.88	46.00
Auto Repair	0.13	0.62	1.98	6.17	20.38	129.00
Car Wash	0.12	0.45	1.63	5.33	17.63	120.50
Recreation	—	0.11	1.02	3.50	5.63	44.00
Bank or C.U.	0.39	1.44	2.59	4.83	6.12	10.00
All Producers' Serv	0.62	4.39	12.20	32.83	91.75	1010.00
Warehousing	—	—	0.37	2.50	13.13	79.00
Farm Equipment	0.12	0.92	2.78	5.50	7.88	34.50
Bulk Fuel	0.18	1.28	2.41	4.33	6.88	11.50
Wholesale	0.17	0.68	2.35	8.67	34.75	544.00
Building Materials	0.14	1.36	3.65	7.17	14.25	68.50
Business Services	—	0.15	0.63	4.67	14.88	272.50
All Producers	0.84	4.25	13.78	39.33	131.63	1146.00
Construction	0.48	2.47	7.74	21.50	70.75	641.00
Manufacturing	0.19	0.96	3.59	11.67	33.88	358.00
Transportation	0.17	0.82	2.46	6.17	27.00	147.00
Doctor*	—	87.00	100.00	100.00	100.00	100.00
Hospital*	—	49.00	91.00	100.00	100.00	100.00
Special Health Care*	—	30.00	96.00	100.00	100.00	100.00
High School*	21.00	89.00	98.00	100.00	100.00	100.00
Grain Elevator*	66.00	94.00	98.00	100.00	100.00	50.00

Note: Values less than 0.10 omitted.

* For these variables the percent of communities offering selected facilities is shown.

new businesses. The growth in urban population and in new businesses was concentrated in centres in the three top functional classifications in both periods, but between 1981 and 1990 the number of communities in these three categories had fallen from thirty-two to sixteen.

In Table 4 the average number of business outlets, by type, are listed for each functional category for 1990. From this information it is clear that the 419 places in the Minimum Convenience category no longer provide a meaningful trade-centre function. There is no single function, private or public, that can be counted on to be present in these places. Full Convenience centres are somewhat better off in that groceries, gasoline, lodging, meals, and financial services are available to consumers in all centres in this category. Farm equipment (although perhaps only one brand-name), bulk fuel, and building materials are available to producers. High schools are present in most

Table 5
Saskatchewan Communities in Top Four Functional Categories: 1990

Partial Shopping Centre		Complete Shopping Centre	Secondary Wholesale-Retail	Primary Wholesale-Retail
Assiniboia	Lanigan	Humboldt	Estevan	Regina
Balcarres	Macklin	Kindersley	Lloydminster	Saskatoon
Battleford	Maidstone	Meadow Lake	Moose Jaw	
Big River	Maple Creek	Melfort	North Battleford	
Biggar	Melville	Nipawin	Prince Albert	
Canora	Moosomin	Tisdale	Swift Current	
Carlyle	Outlook		Weyburn	
Carnduff	Oxbow		Yorkton	
Cudworth	Preeceville			
Davidson	Raymore			
Esterhazy	Redvers			
Eston	Rosetown			
Foam Lake	Rosthern			
Fort Qu'Appelle	Shaunavon			
Gravelbourg	Shellbrook			
Grenfell	Spiritwood			
Gull Lake	St. Walburg			
Hudson Bay	Unity			
Indian Head	Wadena			
Kamsack	Watrous			
Kelvington	Watson			
Kipling	Whitewood			
Langenburg	Wynyard			

communities and health care facilities in some. There are also four producers, on average, in each of these 117 places.

Communities in the top four functional classifications do offer most producer and consumer services. Multiple outlets are usually present as well providing some variety and brand-name choice. Health care and schools are generally available. The majority of the province's producers (83 percent) are also located in the sixty-two places that are included in the top four categories.

In Table 5 the sixty-two communities classified into the top four functional categories in 1990 are listed by name.

5

Trade-Centre Change
by Major Agricultural Regions

Agricultural Areas in Saskatchewan

The viability of communities is determined primarily by the level and stability of the income of the population in the market areas surrounding each centre. In Saskatchewan, the population in the rural areas surrounding these centres is still substantially dependent on agriculture although the degree of this dependence, the mix of crops, and the size of farms differ between the north and the south. To distinguish agricultural regions within the province, special tabulations of 1981 and 1986 census data were obtained from Statistics Canada on all sources of farm gross sales (imputed on the basis of actual sales, prices, and inventories) and all income sources of farm families for the twenty crop-district areas in the province. In addition, the census provides information on cultivated acres and farm size for each crop district. The crop districts were grouped into three agricultural areas according to their position relative to the province in three alternative rating systems as described below.

Variables that formed the basis for rating the crop districts relative to the province were: (1) the percentage of imputed gross agricultural sales that originated from wheat and other small grains, (2) the percentage of imputed gross agricultural sales that originated from other field crops, (3) the percentage of imputed gross agricultural sales that originated from livestock,[1] (4) the imputed gross value of agricultural sales per acre in the crop district, (5) average total acres per farm, and (6) the proportion of aggregate family income that is net farm income. Variables 1, 2, 4, and 6; variables 1, 2, 3, 5, and 6; and variables 1, 2, 3, and 6 were combined to form three alternative methods of rating each crop district relative to the province. The first group (the northern area) is formed by all those crop districts that had aggregate scores above the provincial average in each of the three rating systems.[2] The second group (the southern area) comprises all those crop districts with scores consistently well below the provincial average. The third group (the transition area) contained three crop districts that had mixed ratings in more than one of the rating systems at each point in time and/or through time. The crop districts in each group were aggregated to form the three areas shown in Figure 1.

In 1986 farms in the southern area were roughly 50 percent larger than those in the north, based on cultivated acres, and approximately 63 percent larger based on average total acres. Farm size by agricultural area is shown for census dates between 1961 and 1986 in Table 6. Northern farms, which on average were 59 percent as large as those in the south in 1961, gained somewhat during the following twenty-five years and were 62 percent the size of southern farms in 1986. Intensity of land use increased substantially in the north between these dates however. Cultivated acres rose from 67 percent of the northern land base in 1961 to 77 percent in 1986. In the south, cultivated total acres remained at approximately 70 percent throughout the entire period.

Table 6
Saskatchewan Farm Size (Acres) by Agricultural Area: 1961-1986

	North		South		Transition	
	Total	Cultivated	Total	Cultivated	Total	Cultivated
1961	521	351	887	625	703	556
1971	660	484	1,165	786	827	686
1981	783	600	1,232	881	916	781
1986	854	654	1,388	979	957	817

Source: Census of Canada, special tabulations, various dates.

Community viability is also influenced by other rural economic activity of course. In Saskatchewan other resource-based industry is distributed more or less equally between agricultural areas. Three-quarters of the province's thirty-odd mines are found in the southern and transition areas, and most of the petroleum and natural gas production is accounted for by the south, with only limited amounts in the northern and transition areas. On the other hand, all forest-based activity (several sawmills, two pulp mills) is conducted in the north. There is some tourism in each area, but the majority of the better tourist attractions are in the north. In terms of total employment, the extractive industries together account for a sum that

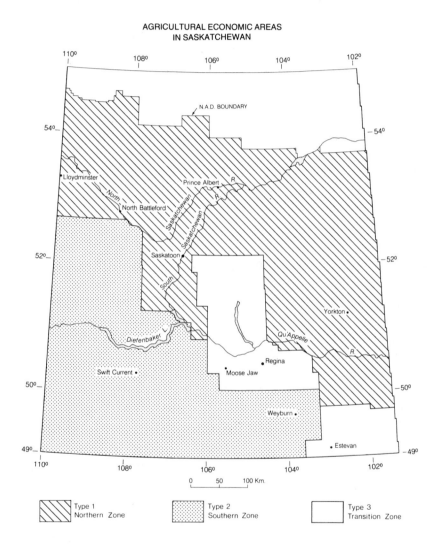

Figure 1. Agricultural Economic Areas in Saskatchewan.

is less than 16 percent of the labour force employed in agriculture. There are no specific estimates for the amount of employment supported by tourism. Nevertheless, except for the few specific sites where mines, mills, or high-quality tourist attractions are situated, the economy of rural Saskatchewan is dominated by agriculture.

Community Change by Agricultural Area

The province's communities are distributed over the three agricultural areas as follows: 51 percent of the communities are in the north, 32 percent in the south, and 17 percent in the transition zone. Throughout the 1961-90 period all but a few of the province's smaller communities experienced decline. Nevertheless, centres in the northern area have realized lower rates of decline than those in the southern area.

Our analysis of community change in this section focusses on the lower four functional classifications which serve the local populations in their respective areas. The analysis proceeds in two ways. First, communities are held in their 1961 classifications (as shown in column 1 of Table 2) and their growth or decline is compared, by area, from 1961 through 1990. Second, the reclassification of communities between 1961 and 1990 is compared, also by area. The first comparison focusses on the experience, through time, of sets of initially similar *communities*, by area. The second comparison indicates how the structure of the trade-centre *system* has changed through time, by area.

Time trends of three summary community-size indicators for the four smallest functional classifications are compared for communities located in the northern and southern areas in Figures 2 to 5. In Figure 2, population, consumers' services, and producers' services in southern communities relative to northern communities are compared for 1961, 1981, and 1990. The lines on these figures represent the ratio of southern to northern mean values at each point in time for the three variables used. The set of northern communities represented here consists of the 125 centres that were classified in the Minimum Convenience category in 1961. The southern set includes the 102 places that were in the same classification in 1961. Figures 3, 4, and 5 are similarly constructed and compare the experience of communities

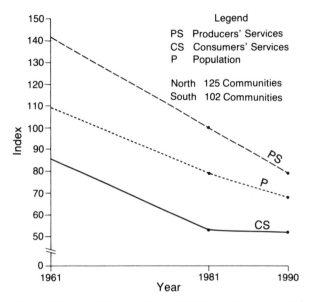

Figure 2. Selected Characteristics of Minimum Convenience Centres: Southern Relative to Northern.

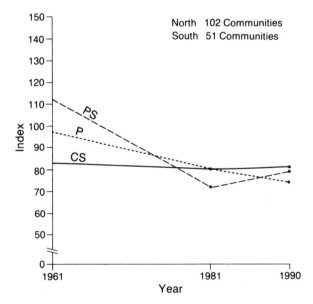

Figure 3. Selected Characteristics of Full Convenience Centres: Southern Relative to Northern.

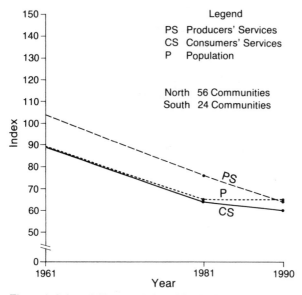

Figure 4. Selected Characteristics of Partial Shopping Centres: Southern Relative to Northern.

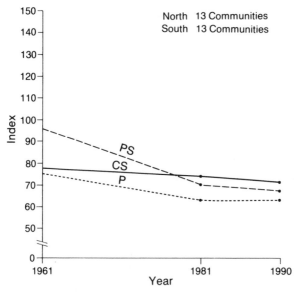

Figure 5. Selected Characteristics of Complete Shopping Centres: Southern Relative to Northern.

in the Full Convenience, Partial Shopping, and Complete Shopping categories, between areas, over the three decades. Although the patterns displayed in these figures differ somewhat in detail between functional classifications, the general patterns are similar and are remarkably consistent. The inescapable conclusion is that southern communities declined substantially relative to their northern counterparts over the three decades included in our analysis. Transition-zone communities are excluded from these figures in the interest of space. Tables 7, 8, and 9 compare changes in northern with southern communities in detail at each date of the study.

In our second comparison, changes in the structure of the trade-centre system between areas are identified. In Table 10 the proportion of communities in each functional category at the beginning of the period which subsequently declined in status (D), retained its status (S), or rose (G) is shown by area. Rates of decline in the south consistently exceed those in the north for all functional categories between 1961 and 1990. For the subperiods, southern communities declined more rapidly than those in the north during the relatively prosperous 1961-81 period as well as during the less prosperous 1981-90 period. Only one instance can be identified in which decline in the north exceeded that in the south. This is for the Full Convenience category between 1981 and 1990.

A final perspective is provided in Table 11 which focusses on the shifting areal concentration of all communities within the trade-centre hierarchy. In this table the proportion of the province's communities classified in the top three (four) functional categories is identified, by area, for each of the three dates used in this analysis. Consistent with previous observations, the share of the province's viable communities in the north is shown to increase over time and decrease in the south, based on either the top three or the top four functional classifications.

Table 7
Difference Profile: 1961

Means of the Clusters in the Northern Zone Minus
the Means of the Clusters in the Southern Zone

Cluster	MC	FC	PS	CS
Population	**-10.02**	**7.61**	**78.22**	**634.32**
Construction	0.00	0.10	0.41	1.95
Manufacturing	0.02	0.00	0.20	1.12
Transportation	0.00	0.04	-0.12	0.13
All Producers	**0.01**	**0.14**	**0.49**	**3.19**
Warehousing	0.00	0.00	0.00	0.06
Farm Equipment	-0.15	-0.36	-0.32	-0.68
Bulk Fuel	-0.08	-0.24	-0.21	-0.02
Wholesale	0.00	0.00	0.00	1.12
Building Materials	-0.07	0.14	0.26	0.02
Business Services	0.00	0.00	0.00	0.00
All Producers' Serv	**-0.30**	**-0.46**	**-0.26**	**0.50**
General Store	0.41	0.92	1.04	1.21
Grocery Store	0.11	-0.09	0.16	2.03
Special Food	-0.03	0.14	0.58	0.21
Auto Sales	-0.07	-0.39	-0.42	-0.27
Gas Station	0.22	0.52	0.55	3.41
Clothing Store	0.00	0.08	-0.09	0.00
Furniture Store	0.00	0.04	0.01	0.17
Home Furnishings	-0.01	-0.15	-0.18	0.35
Restaurant	0.02	0.07	0.82	1.45
Drug Store	-0.02	0.07	-0.02	0.22
Special Retail	-0.05	-0.12	0.05	1.30
Credit Agency	0.00	0.01	0.00	0.00
Hotel	0.18	0.05	-0.05	0.95
Laundries	0.00	0.00	-0.05	-0.09
Personal Services	0.02	0.14	-0.03	1.13
Auto Repair	-0.20	-0.01	-0.59	-1.15
Car Wash	-0.01	0.44	0.11	1.16
Recreation	0.05	0.18	0.28	0.05
Banks and C.U.	-0.02	-0.07	0.03	0.47
All Consumers' Serv	**0.59**	**1.82**	**2.20**	**12.59**
Doctors	0.01	0.04	-0.14	0.00
Hospitals	0.00	-0.07	-0.13	0.00
Special Care	0.00	0.01	0.01	0.27
High School	-0.05	-0.08	0.04	0.00
Elevator	0.00	0.00	0.00	0.00

(Grouped on 1961 Cluster)

Table 8
Difference Profile: 1981

Means of the Clusters in the Northern Zone Minus
the Means of the Clusters in the Southern Zone

Cluster	MC	FC	PS	CS
Population	**18.56**	**60.88**	**296.60**	**1183.43**
Construction	0.14	0.52	3.10	4.19
Manufacturing	0.09	0.16	0.82	2.78
Transportation	0.03	-0.04	0.52	2.05
All Producers	**0.26**	**0.64**	**4.43**	**9.02**
Warehousing	0.00	0.00	0.00	0.78
Farm Equipment	0.02	0.02	0.11	-0.27
Bulk Fuel	-0.02	0.11	0.22	0.90
Wholesale	0.00	0.00	0.00	1.89
Building Materials	0.01	0.26	0.67	1.69
Business Services	0.00	0.00	0.00	0.35
All Producers' Serv	**0.01**	**0.39**	**0.99**	**5.34**
General Store	0.20	0.12	0.60	1.25
Grocery Store	0.05	0.12	0.73	2.13
Special Food	-0.01	0.03	0.09	1.71
Auto Sales	0.00	0.04	0.43	0.84
Gas Station	0.25	0.44	0.15	2.53
Clothing Store	-0.01	0.02	0.58	-0.32
Furniture Store	-0.01	0.04	0.15	0.60
Home Furnishings	0.03	0.02	0.49	0.21
Restaurant	0.08	0.17	0.71	0.10
Drug Store	0.00	0.00	0.21	0.88
Special Retail	-0.01	0.03	0.30	2.59
Credit Agency	0.00	0.01	0.00	-0.36
Hotel	0.11	0.01	0.37	0.47
Laundries	-0.01	0.01	-0.03	0.66
Personal Services	0.00	0.00	-0.05	0.77
Auto Repair	0.05	-0.01	0.24	1.11
Car Wash	0.06	0.08	0.19	2.67
Recreation	0.01	-0.01	0.14	0.52
Banks And C.U.	0.00	-0.06	0.08	0.52
All Consumers' Serv	**0.78**	**1.05**	**5.39**	**18.88**
Doctors	0.00	0.04	-0.24	0.00
Hospitals	0.00	0.05	-0.18	0.00
Special Care	0.00	0.03	0.15	0.00
High School	-0.04	-0.05	0.09	0.00
Elevator	-0.21	-0.08	-0.02	-0.07

(Grouped on 1961 Cluster)

Table 9
Difference Profile: 1990

Means of the Clusters in the Northern Zone Minus
the Means of the Clusters in the Southern Zone

Cluster	MC	FC	PS	CS
Population	**28.83**	**84.12**	**300.77**	**1294.31**
Construction	0.04	0.48	1.88	3.60
Manufacturing	0.06	0.27	1.24	2.54
Transportation	-0.01	-0.01	0.45	1.40
All Producers	**0.09**	**0.75**	**3.57**	**7.55**
Warehousing	-0.01	-0.02	0.13	0.53
Farm Equipment	0.03	-0.10	0.56	-0.34
Bulk Fuel	0.00	-0.04	0.23	1.00
Wholesale	0.04	0.25	0.46	3.04
Building Materials	0.01	0.31	0.83	1.81
Business Services	0.00	0.06	0.14	1.08
All Producers' Serv	**0.06**	**0.46**	**2.35**	**7.12**
General Store	0.11	0.21	0.42	0.40
Grocery Store	0.01	0.15	1.07	0.74
Special Food	0.00	0.11	0.39	1.65
Auto Sales	0.01	0.02	0.40	0.69
Gas Station	0.16	0.41	0.29	1.70
Clothing Store	0.02	0.11	0.52	2.43
Furniture Store	0.00	0.04	0.21	0.65
Home Furnishings	0.01	-0.10	0.29	0.02
Restaurant	0.07	0.10	1.36	3.10
Drug Store	0.00	-0.03	0.13	1.53
Special Retail	0.00	0.14	0.30	2.34
Credit Agency	0.10	0.25	0.76	3.20
Hotel	0.16	-0.20	0.74	0.80
Laundries	0.01	0.00	0.07	0.26
Personal Services	0.00	0.03	0.22	0.80
Auto Repair	0.09	0.03	0.46	0.37
Car Wash	0.03	0.10	0.32	1.23
Recreation	0.00	0.07	0.29	1.22
Banks and C.U.	0.07	-0.14	0.23	0.64
All Consumers' Serv	**0.84**	**1.28**	**8.4**	**23.76**
Doctors	0.01	0.07	-0.06	0.00
Hospitals	0.00	0.01	-0.13	0.00
Special Care	0.00	0.07	0.26	0.00
High School	-0.04	-0.11	0.11	0.00
Elevator	-0.12	-0.15	-0.02	-0.07

(Grouped on 1961 Cluster)

Table 10
Proportion of Communities Declining, Remaining Stable, or Growing by Period

Economic Area	MCC*			FCC			PSC			CSC			SWR			PWR		
	D	S	G	D	S	G	D	S	G	D	S	G	D	S	G	D	S	G
1961-1990																		
North	–	98	2	69	29	2	70	30	–	64	36	–	–	100	–	–	100	–
South	–	100	–	73	27	–	96	4	–	92	8	–	–	100	–	–	–	–
Trans	–	100	–	83	17	–	68	32	–	100	–	–	–	100	–	–	100	–
1961 - 1981																		
North	–	98	2	64	36	–	71	27	2	–	100	–	–	100	–	–	100	–
South	–	100	–	73	27	–	92	8	–	46	54	–	–	100	–	–	–	–
Trans	–	100	–	72	28	–	74	26	–	100	–	–	–	100	–	–	100	–
1981 - 1990																		
North	–	94	6	27	65	8	20	80	–	67	33	–	–	100	–	–	100	–
South	–	97	3	14	83	3	62	38	–	86	14	–	–	100	–	–	–	–
Trans	–	97	3	46	50	4	–	100	–	–	–	–	–	100	–	–	100	–

*The indication of stability at the Minimum Convenience level is somewhat misleading because there is no lower classification to which these centres could descend. In absolute terms the majority of communities initially in this classification subsequently lost both population and business outlets.

Table 11
Number and Percent of High Level Centres in Each Economic Area
1961, 1981, and 1990

Economic	A. Top Three Functional Categories					
	1961		1981		1990	
Area	No.	%	No.	%	No.	%
North	19	49	20	63	10	63
South	15	38	9	28	3	19
Trans	5	13	3	9	3	19
Total	39	100	32	100	16	100
	B. Top Four Functional Categories					
Economic	1961		1981		1990	
Area	No.	%	No.	%	No.	%
North	75	54	35	56	38	61
South	39	28	17	27	13	21
Trans	24	17	10	16	11	18
Total	138	100	62	100	62	100

Other Factors Affecting Community Viability

A review of Tables 7-9 reveals several interesting structural differences between the four lower level categories of northern and southern communities. Southern communities, for example, were more specialized in serving the agricultural industry in 1961 than their northern counterparts. In general, southern centres had greater numbers of farm equipment, bulk fuel, for-hire transport, automobile (truck) sales, and auto (truck) repair outlets. Northern communities, on the other hand, had somewhat larger populations in 1961 (except for the Minimum Convenience category), a modestly greater number of manufacturing firms, and better developed consumer-service sectors. No systematic differences were apparent in the provision of public infrastructure.

Following 1961, northern communities increased their initial advantage in manufacturing, developed a complement of producers' services around their growing manufacturing industries, and expanded their consumer-service activities. Between 1961 and 1990 the northern area gained 268 manufacturing plants outside the largest city, while the southern area gained only seventy. Southern communities did not diversify and their agricultural-service and consumer-service industries contracted as agricultural consolidation reduced the number of farms. Although services to agriculture declined in the north, the contraction was not as rapid as in the south. Thus, by the end of the period southern communities no longer demonstrated a relative dominance even in their former specialization. With little or no alternative development to offset the consolidation in agriculture, the population of southern Minimum Convenience, Full Convenience, and Partial Shopping centres declined. In the north, on the other hand, only Minimum Convenience centres experienced a loss of population.

It is of interest to note that the first and second largest relative gains by northern communities were in producers and population, except for Complete Shopping centres where producers' services recorded the largest relative gain. While consumers' services did increase in the north relative to the south, the relative gains were less than gains in population. The implication is that the growth of population and income did not translate into proportionate increases in local consumer expenditures. It may be further noted that changes in public infrastructure did not parallel changes in commercial functions. The pattern of modest public infrastructure differences noted in 1961 is basically still the same in 1990. The privately owned elevator system, on the other hand, does reflect a differential adjustment. Southern grain-dependent communities have retained a higher proportion of these facilities.

While the expansion of manufacturing in the north can be attributed, in part, to the more diversified agriculture practiced there, a contributing influence can very likely be associated with widening differences in population densities. Between 1961 and 1990 the population of the northern area increased by 12 percent compared with a decline in the south of 23 percent, as shown in Table 12. It should be noted that population changes recorded in this table do not follow precisely the classifications of trade centres used elsewhere in this report because of the way in which the primary population data are organized. The first category, cities, includes only the Primary and Secondary Wholesale-Retail centres. The second category, "other organized," includes all communities in our bottom four classifications and, in addition, the populations of a few small places which were under fifty in 1961 and were thus excluded from our study. The final category, "unorganized," refers essentially to rural areas but does include a few small unorganized hamlets.

Table 12
Population Change by Agricultural Areas: 1961-1990

North	Date				Change	
	1961	1971	1981	1990	Absolute	Percent
Cities	152,272	195,094	231,750	266,626	114,354	75
Other Organized	104,024	112,065	123,172	127,430	23,406	23
Unorganized	207,861	161,762	141,152	125,984	-81,887	-39
Totals	464,157	468,921	496,074	520,040	55,883	12
South	Date				Change	
	1961	1971	1981	1990	Absolute	Percent
Cities	21,287	24,230	24,270	25,358	4,071	19
Other Organized	62,425	59,590	56,895	55,307	-7,118	-11
Unorganized	89,561	76,329	60,654	53,180	-36,381	-41
Totals	173,273	160,149	141,819	133,845	-39,428	-23
Transition	Date				Change	
	1961	1971	1981	1990	Absolute	Percent
Cities	153,075	180,473	206,102	192,610	39,535	26
Other Organized	32,449	33,654	37,404	38,759	6,310	19
Unorganized	55,483	42,734	36,850	32,839	-22,644	-41
Totals	241,007	256,861	280,356	264,208	23,201	10

In 1961, there were 3.42 people per square mile in the south, outside of the Wholesale-Retail centres, 67 percent of the northern figure which was 5.08. By 1990, the southern figure had fallen to 2.44, 59 percent of the northern figure of 4.13. The potential for production for local markets, initially less attractive in the south, worsened over the period under study. In addition, the possibility of being able to recruit a local labour force was obviously lower in the south at the beginning of the period and also declined with the passage of time. By 1990 the area from which a potential employer would have to draw to recruit a labour force of a given size in the south was nearly 70 percent larger than that required in the north.

NOTES

1. Livestock sales excluded beef cattle because it was not possible to distinguish cow-calf operations, which require relatively little labour, from feeder-cattle operations which are somewhat more labour intensive.

2. For variables 2, 3, and 4 the ratio was formed with the crop-district value in the numerator and the provincial average in the denominator. That is, a proportion of sales originating from other crops or from livestock in excess of the provincial average is considered to make a positive contribution to the economic viability of communities in that district. Likewise, an above-average sales per acre was considered a positive attribute. For the other three variables (percent of total sales originating from wheat and small grains, net farm income as a percentage of aggregate family income, and farm size) the provincial average was the numerator and the value for the crop district was the denominator. In the first instance, heavy concentration in wheat and small grains represents an absence of diversification that leaves the area more vulnerable to long-term decreases in the prices of these commodities and more likely to pursue very land-extensive agriculture. In the case of net farm income as a percentage of aggregate family income, a score for the crop district above the provincial average was considered a negative attribute because it represents a lack of diversification of farm-family labour into alternative (nonfarm) uses. A larger than average farm size was also considered a negative attribute because of the implications for size of farm population and thus community support.

6

Shopping Patterns and Market Areas

Introduction

Previous studies of shopping habits of Saskatchewan's rural residents defined a pattern in which a high percentage of everyday goods and services were purchased in the nearest community. Higher-order and specialized products were purchased in either the larger regional centres or in the province's major cities (Saskatchewan, 1957; Stabler and Williams, 1973).

As a part of the present study of the rural economy, questionnaires were sent to farm families across the province in the spring of 1991. The discussion of shopping patterns and market areas in the following section of this chapter is based on 438 questionnaires returned by these rural residents.

Overview of 1991 Shopping Patterns

In general, respondents indicated that common, everyday goods and services are obtained as close to home as possible, as was the case in the survey reported in Stabler and Williams (1973). Compared with twenty years ago, however, fewer items are available in lower-level centres. Consequently, the closest outlet for some items is farther away, on average, than was the case in the early 1970s. In addition, rural dwellers have shifted their demands for some items to higher-level centres. Thus a higher proportion of some products are now obtained from larger centres than was the case in the 1972 study even though these items might still be available in closer centres. For such items rural dwellers are expressing a preference for greater variety and price competition over convenience and are prepared to travel farther to satisfy these desires.

Another pattern clearly revealed in the returned questionnaires is that shopping is conducted on a multi-tiered basis by those living near the communities in the three lowest functional categories. For respondents living adjacent to Complete Shopping and Secondary Wholesale-Retail centres, shopping patterns are two-tiered. For this

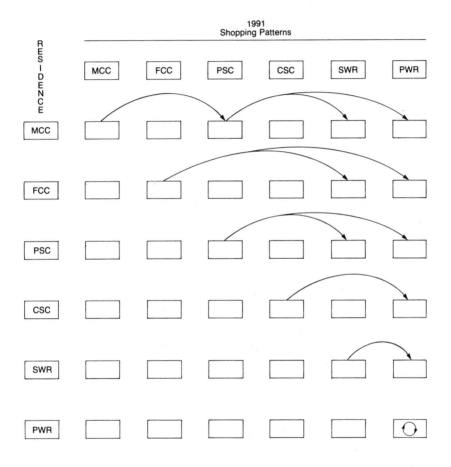

Figure 6. Shopping Patterns of Rural Residents by Proximity of Residence to Class of Trade Centre.

latter group of people, most products are obtained in their home community with some highly specialized services obtained in the province's two largest cities. People living in or near Saskatoon and Regina obtain virtually all of their goods and services in these cities.

Throughout the range of the hierarchy, Saskatoon and Regina stand out as important providers of high-order consumer goods such as specialized medical and hospital services, clothing, shoes, and furniture.

Finally, bypassing of opportunities to purchase, en route to higher order centres, is common and occurs at all levels of the hierarchy. A generalized summary of the 1991 shopping patterns is provided in Figure 6.

Detailed Analysis of 1991 Shopping Patterns

On the questionnaires sent out in the spring of 1991, respondents were asked to identify their residence by the community closest to their home. They were then asked to identify the community in which they obtained a list of the thirty-one goods and services listed. These data were subsequently arranged to provide the information in the cells of a matrix like that generalized in Figure 6. When the matrix is read across one of the rows, it portrays the shopping pattern of people living in or near communities of the type identified in the first cell of that row. Entries opposite the cell marked FCC in row two, for example, identify the shopping pattern of people living in or near Full Convenience centres.

Minimum Convenience Centres

Tables 13, 14, and 15 identify the percentage of each of the thirty-one goods and services obtained by category of centre in which the item was acquired.

In Table 13 the percentages of each item obtained in Minimum Convenience centres (the home community) and in Full Convenience centres is shown. For only three items is more than 50 percent of the total obtained in the home community. These are the services of the post office, the grain elevator and elementary schools. Between one-third and one-half of the requirements for an additional six items

Table 13
Shopping Patterns of Rural Residents Living
Near Minimum Convenience Centres: 1991

Classification of Community in Which Item is Obtained			
Minimum Convenience Centre		Full Convenience Centre	
Item	%	Item	%
Post Office	75	Bank or Credit Union	17
Grain Elevator	72	Bulk Fuel	17
Elementary School	65	High School	16
High School	46	Insurance	15
Bulk Fuel	40	Physician, General	15
Gasoline	38	Gasoline	14
Bank or Credit Union	34	Elementary School	14
Recreation/Entertainment	34	Beer or Spirits	13
Insurance	33	Hospital	11
Auto, Repair	31	Real Estate Agent	11
Groceries	26	Hardware	10
Barber/Beauty Salon	22	Auto, Repair	9
Hardware	20	Farm Equipment, Repait	9
Beer or Spirits	19	Grain Elevator	9
Real Estate Agent	17	Building Materials	9
Farm Equipment, Repair	16	Accounting/Legal	8
Building Material	14	Barber/Beauty Salon	8
Restaurant	10	Drugs & Toiletries	8
Farm Equipment, Purchase	9	Recreation/Entertainment	8
Auto, New or Used	8	Farm Equipment, Purchase	7
Dry Cleaning/Laundry	6	Groceries	7
Accounting/Legal	6	Restaurant	6
Drugs & Toiletries	5	Post Office	5
Home Furnishings	5	Auto, New or Used	5
Furniture	5	Home Furnishings	3
Physician, Specialist	5	Furniture	3
Shoes	5	Dry Cleaning/Laundry	3
Clothing	4	Shoes	2
Hospital	4	Physician, Specialist	2
Dentist	4	Dentist	2
Physician, General	3	Clothing	2

are also satisfied by the home communities. These are high school, bulk fuel, gasoline, bank or credit union, recreation and insurance.

These statistics provide another perspective on the trade-centre role of Saskatchewan's 419 Minimum Convenience centres. Of the four items most frequently utilized in these communities, three are publically provided infrastructure. The fourth, perhaps properly described as private infrastructure, is the grain elevator. Nothing sold

Table 14
Shopping Patterns of Rural Residents Living
Near Minimum Convenience Centres: 1991

Classification of Community in Which Item is Obtained

Partial Shopping Centre		Complete Shopping Centre	
Item	%	Item	%
Real Estate Agent	28	Dry Cleaning/Laundry	15
Physician, General	27	Farm Equipment, Purchase	13
Beer or Spirits	24	Dentist	13
Hospital	24	Farm Equipment, Repair	12
Farm Equipment, Repair	21	Hardware	12
Farm Equipment, Purchase	21	Clothing	11
Barber/Beauty Salon	21	Building Materials	11
Insurance	21	Physician, General	10
Building Materials	21	Auto, New or Used	10
Dentist	20	Beer or Spirits	10
Accounting/Legal	20	Accounting/Legal	10
Dry Cleaning/Laundry	20	Shoes	10
Auto, Repair	19	Hospital	10
High School	19	Groceries	10
Drugs & Toiletries	18	Bank or Credit Union	9
Gasoline	18	Drugs & Toiletries	9
Auto, New or Used	18	Restaurant	9
Bulk Fuel	18	Auto, Repair	9
Groceries	17	Furniture	8
Hardware	16	Barber/Beauty Salon	8
Bank or Credit Union	16	Home Furnishings	8
Recreation/Entertainment	16	Recreation/Entertainment	7
Restaurant	14	Insurance	7
Elementary School	13	Bulk Fuel	6
Home Furnishings	12	Gasoline	5
Clothing	12	High School	5
Shoes	9	Real Estate Agent	5
Furniture	9	Physician, Specialist	3
Post Office	7	Elementary School	3
Grain Elevator	7	Post Office	3
Physician, Specialist	2	Grain Elevator	2

at retail satisfies more than 40 percent of the residents' needs. In fact, for two-thirds of the items on the list, three-quarters of the residents' demands are satisfied outside the home community.

Turning to transactions away from the home community, residents of Minimum Convenience centres depend very little on communities in the next highest category — the 117 Full Convenience centres. While a few items are acquired in communities next higher in the

Table 15
Shopping Patterns of Rural Residents Living
Near Minimum Convenience Centres: 1991

Classification of Community in Which Item is Obtained

Secondary Wholesale-Retail		Primary Wholesale-Retail	
Item	%	Item	%
Drugs & Toiletries	43	Physician, Specialist	61
Furniture	39	Furniture	36
Shoes	38	Shoes	36
Clothing	37	Home Furnishings	35
Home Furnishings	36	Clothing	34
Dentist	36	Restaurant	28
Dry Cleaning/Laundry	35	Accounting/Legal	26
Auto, New or Used	35	Dentist	26
Farm Equipment, Purchase	33	Hospital	24
Restaurant	33	Auto, New or Used	24
Building Materials	31	Dry Cleaning/Laundry	22
Accounting/Legal	29	Physician, General	19
Farm Equipment, Repair	28	Farm Equipment, Purchase	17
Hospital	27	Barber/Beauty Salon	16
Hardware	26	Drugs & Toiletries	16
Physician, General	26	Hardware	15
Real Estate Agent	26	Groceries	15
Physician, Specialist	26	Recreation/Entertainment	15
Groceries	26	Building Materials	14
Barber/Beauty Salon	25	Farm Equipment, Repair	14
Auto, Repair	22	Beer or Spirits	13
Beer or Spirits	21	Real Estate Agent	13
Recreation/Entertainment	20	Auto, Repair	10
Insurance	16	Gasoline	10
Bank or Credit Union	16	Insurance	9
Bulk Fuel	14	Bank or Credit Union	8
Gasoline	14	Bulk Fuel	5
High School	12	Grain Elevator	3
Grain Elevator	7	Post Office	3
Post Office	6	High School	2
Elementary School	4	Elementary School	2

functional classification, only three of thirty-one items are obtained
with greater frequency in Full Convenience than in Partial Shopping
centres (Table 14). For residents of Minimum Convenience centres,
the utilization of banking or credit union facilities, elementary
schools, and grain elevators in Full Convenience centres marginally
exceed the utilization of these facilities in Partial Shopping centres
(17 percent versus 16, 14 versus 13, and 9 versus 7 respectively).

Clearly, Full Convenience centres are bypassed in favour of Partial Shopping centres.

In Table 14 purchases in Partial and Complete Shopping centres are recorded. It would appear that Partial Shopping centres share the role of the home community with Minimum Convenience centres for those rural residents living near the latter type communities. Home communities provide the basic infrastructure while Partial Shopping centres share in the role of providing some common trade and services at the retail level. One-fifth or more of the requirements for twelve common goods and services are satisfied in Partial Shopping centres.

As noted, Full Convenience centres are bypassed in frequenting Partial Shopping centres. Similarly, Complete Shopping centres are bypassed when purchases are made still further up the hierarchy. Only two items, specialist physician services and shoes, are obtained with greater frequency in Complete Shopping than in Partial Shopping centres. This latter observation does need to be qualified, however, by recalling that there were only six centres in Saskatchewan classified as Complete Shopping centres in 1990. Thus, most rural residents would be closer to one of the Wholesale-Retail centres than to a Complete Shopping centre.

Table 15 records purchases made in Secondary and Primary Wholesale-Retail Centres. Clearly both types of communities play a major role in the shopping behaviour of rural residents. Over 50 percent of the requirements for thirteen higher-order goods and services are satisfied in one of the province's ten cities. Saskatoon and Regina dominate in the provision of specialist physician services while the Secondary Wholesale-Retail centres dominate in the provision of other high-order items. Between 40 and 50 percent of purchases made for six additional items are made in the ten Wholesale-Retail centres. Thus over 40 percent of the requirements for nineteen of the thirty-one goods and services for which information was requested are satisfied in the province's ten largest communities.

Full Convenience Centres

An abbreviated version of the shopping patterns of rural dwellers living near Full Convenience centres is shown in Table 16. This pattern differs from that of rural dwellers living near Minimum Convenience centres in that people living near Full Convenience centres are able to utilize their home communities to a much greater extent to satisfy requirements for everyday goods and services. In this case, over 50 percent of their needs for fifteen of the thirty-one items is satisfied in home communities. Between one-third and one-half of their purchases of four additional items are also made in the centre closest to their residence.

When the local community is unable to satisfy their needs, rural dwellers living near Full Convenience centres depend almost exclusively on the province's Wholesale-Retail centres, bypassing both Partial and Complete Shopping Centres along the way. The ten communities in the Wholesale-Retail categories provide over 40 percent of the demand for fourteen of the thirty-one items and between one-third and 40 percent for four additional items. Even for goods and services obtained primarily in the home community, substantial fractions of the demand for these items are satisfied in the ten largest centres, reflecting the purchase of even everyday goods and services in the large centres whenever a trip is made to obtain a more specialized product.

A few transactions are conducted in centres at other levels of the hierarchy, of course, as reflected by the fact that none of the entries in the total column sum to 100 percent. Farm equipment and automobile purchases are made in Partial Shopping centres (26 and 17 percent respectively) and dentists' services are obtained in both Partial and Complete Shopping centres (15 and 11 percent). Between 10 and 15 percent of seven other items are also obtained in Partial Shopping centres (building materials, farm equipment repair, hospital, accounting/legal services, dry cleaning, drugs and toiletries, and hardware).

One additional observation is worthy of note. Saskatoon and Regina were the primary providers only of specialized physicians' services for residents of Minimum Convenience centres. However,

Table 16
Shopping Patterns of Rural Residents Living
Near Full Convenience Centres: 1991

	Classification of Community in Which Item is Obtained			
Item	FCC (%)	SWR (%)	PWR (%)	Total (%)
Elementary School	91	2	1	94
High School	91	1	0	92
Post Office	89	2	3	94
Grain Elevator	82	2	3	87
Insurance	81	5	5	91
Bulk Fuel	79	7	4	90
Gasoline	76	8	6	90
Physician, General	74	7	10	91
Bank or Credit Union	68	12	7	87
Beer or Spirits	65	9	13	87
Groceries	61	15	13	89
Real Estate Agent	61	27	6	94
Recreation/Entertainment	61	11	18	90
Auto, Repair	58	14	13	85
Barber/Beauty Salon	54	17	18	89
Drugs & Toiletries	46	20	17	83
Hardware	45	21	17	83
Building Materials	41	22	19	82
Hospital	38	17	27	82
Restaurant	31	29	26	86
Auto, New or Used	29	26	22	77
Farm Equipment, Purchase	27	27	14	68
Farm Equipment, Repair	26	11	47	84
Dry Cleaning/Laundry	25	34	20	79
Accounting/Legal	23	27	30	80
Dentist	8	32	33	73
Clothing	8	34	42	84
Furniture	7	34	44	85
Home Furnishings	5	37	43	85
Physician, Specialist	4	23	70	97
Shoes	2	37	45	84

these two major cities dominate in the provision of nine of the fourteen products for which the top two tiers (Secondary plus Primary Wholesale-Retail centres) serve over 40 percent of the demand by residents of Full Convenience centres. This observation summarizes a pattern that is evident at all levels in the hierarchy; that is, the higher the functional classification of the home community the further up the hierarchy one goes to satisfy requirements not met by the home community.

Partial Shopping Centres

Continuing the trend evident at the Full Convenience level, rural dwellers living near Partial Shopping centres rely even more on their home communities for everyday goods and services. As a group, these forty-six communities satisfy over 50 percent of the local demand for twenty-six of thirty-one goods and services. For twenty-one of the study items these centres provide 70 percent or more of the local requirements.

Table 17
Shopping Patterns of Rural Residents Living
Near Partial Shopping Centres: 1991

Item	Classification of Community in Which Item is Obtained			
	PSC (%)	SWR (%)	PWR (%)	Total (%)
Grain Elevator	94	0	0	94
Post Office	94	0	0	94
Elementary School	94	0	0	94
High School	94	0	0	94
Real Estate Agent	93	0	7	100
Beer or Spirits	89	6	4	99
Insurance	87	0	5	92
Bank or Credit Union	86	3	3	92
Bulk Fuel	83	1	2	86
Gasoline	83	1	4	88
Physician, General	83	6	8	97
Auto, Repair	82	11	2	95
Barber/Beauty Salon	81	8	4	93
Groceries	78	7	8	93
Drugs & Toiletries	76	14	7	97
Hospital	73	10	13	96
Recreation/Entertainment	73	6	18	97
Building Materials	72	19	5	96
Dry Cleaning/Laundry	70	11	16	97
Farm Equipment, Repair	70	14	6	90
Hardware	70	16	11	97
Farm Equipment, Purchase	67	24	2	93
Accounting/Legal	65	16	19	100
Dentist	57	23	16	96
Restaurant	55	18	25	98
Auto, New or Used	54	24	15	93
Clothing	37	31	29	97
Furniture	31	34	35	100
Shoes	30	37	31	98
Home Furnishings	30	34	36	100
Physician, Specialist	6	26	68	100

Virtually everything purchased outside the home community is obtained in the ten Wholesale-Retail centres as indicated in the totals column of Table 17. Only two entries in this column sum to less than 90 percent — gasoline and bulk fuel; 10 percent of the former and 11 percent of the latter are purchased from outlets in Minimum Convenience centres.

Needless to say, Complete Shopping centres are bypassed by rural dwellers living near Partial Shopping centres in favour of one of the province's largest ten communities. There are only three items for which purchases from Complete Shopping centres are non-zero. These are automobile purchases, at 3 percent; and farm equipment purchases and repairs, each at 1 percent.

For all goods and services obtained in the Wholesale-Retail centres, Saskatoon and Regina dominated the other eight communities, fourteen items to twelve. For those items where 30 percent or more of the demand was supplied by Wholesale-Retail centres, Saskatoon and Regina marginally dominated the other eight, five to four.

Complete Shopping Centres

At the Complete Shopping centre level, over 65 percent of the demand for twenty-nine of thirty-one items is satisfied in home communities. As Table 18 indicates, only shoes and specialist physician services are obtained in equal or greater quantities outside home communities.

Of the goods and services acquired elsewhere, nearly all are provided by the Wholesale-Retail centres, with Saskatoon and Regina clearly dominating this trade. Only two items, farm equipment purchases and farm equipment repair depart from this pattern. These purchases are spread across several levels.

The bypassing phenomenon is once again observed. Of the nineteen items showing some sales in the Wholesale-Retail centres, Saskatoon and Regina dominate in sixteen cases.

Wholesale-Retail Centres

As could well be expected, rural dwellers living near Secondary

Table 18
Shopping Patterns of Rural Residents Living
Near Complete Shopping Centres: 1991

Item	Classification of Community in Which Item is Obtained			
	CSC (%)	SWR (%)	PWR (%)	Total (%)
Dry Cleaning/Laundry	100	0	0	100
Insurance	100	0	0	100
Real Estate Agent	100	0	0	100
High School	100	0	0	100
Elementary School	100	0	0	100
Grain Elevator	100	0	0	100
Gasoline	100	0	0	100
Beer or Spirits	100	0	0	100
Bank or Credit Union	100	0	0	100
Post Office	100	0	0	100
Groceries	98	0	2	100
Bulk Fuel	98	0	2	100
Drugs & Toiletries	96	1	3	99
Accounting/Legal	95	0	5	100
Auto, Repair	94	5	1	100
Auto, New or Used	92	0	0	92
Barber/Beauty Salon	90	10	0	100
Building Materials	90	3	7	100
Hardware	89	2	9	100
Physician, General	88	10	2	100
Farm Equipment, Repair	85	0	1	86
Recreation/Entertainment	85	1	14	100
Restaurant	81	5	14	100
Dentist	80	3	13	96
Farm Equipment, Purchase	76	0	0	76
Hospital	73	10	17	100
Clothing	67	12	21	100
Furniture	65	6	29	100
Home Furnishings	65	6	29	100
Physician, Specialist	50	0	50	100
Shoes	44	12	44	100

Wholesale-Retail centres are able to satisfy virtually all of their needs from their home communities. Saskatoon and Regina are depended upon for only hospital services (19 percent) and specialist physician services (62 percent). Nine additional items are obtained in small quantities (2 to 5 percent) from Saskatoon and Regina. These are the conventional high-order items such as clothing, shoes, furniture, home furnishings, and hardware, or entertainment such as recreation and dining out. Dentists' services and building materials complete the list.

Rural residents living near Saskatoon and Regina do not depend upon any other Saskatchewan communities for any goods or services.

A Qualifying Note

Our survey was sent only to farmers living in rural areas. As such, the results can only reflect their tastes and shopping patterns. It does not seem too likely, however, that farmers' shopping patterns would differ much from those who lived in small rural communities.

At some point, business and professional people living in the larger rural communities may have tastes and, therefore, shopping habits which do differ from farm families. Such differences, if they exist, would likely reflect an even more urban orientation than revealed in the preceding tables.

A second qualification is that our results do not reflect out-of-province shopping patterns. It is common knowledge, for example, that shopping excursions to the West Edmonton Mall are systematically organized in Saskatoon and Regina. It is also known that Saskatchewan residents living near the Alberta border will purchase goods and services in that province from time to time in order to avoid the Saskatchewan provincial sales tax. Cross-border shopping into the United States affects retail sales in some southern Saskatchewan communities. How important such shopping trips are as a fraction of the total, however, is not known.

Finally, our data do not reflect business transactions for sectors other than agriculture. Nevertheless, the concentration of over 80 percent of the province's wholesale outlets in the ten Wholesale-Retail centres ensures that the pattern of all commercial transactions would be highly focussed on these ten cities. Saskatoon and Regina together account for 65 percent of the province's wholesale outlets. Since rural communities would not be able to satisfy even a small fraction of their wholesale requirements, the pattern of wholesale transactions would be even more dominated by the ten cities than in the case of consumer markets and farm business transactions.

Market Areas

The questionnaires used to collect information on shopping patterns also recorded distances travelled to obtain the thirty-one goods and services used in the survey. These distances can be taken as approximate market areas for those items traded between levels in the hierarchy.

Saskatoon and Regina provide a collection of high-order goods and services to residents of much of the province. Specialist physicians' services, furniture, home furnishings, shoes, clothing, hospital services, and some types of entertainment are obtained in the two major cities by people throughout the province. Thus the size of the market area for these high-order items would be very large. Their market areas for gasoline, groceries, bulk fuel, or elementary school services would be considerably smaller, however.

For the smaller communities, very little is traded between levels. Thus distances recorded for travel to Minimum and Full Convenience centres reflects primarily the distance that rural dwellers drive to obtain the common everyday goods and services provided in these communities.

Table 19
Distances Travelled by Rural Dwellers to Shop
by Functional Classification of Centre: 1991

| Functional | Average Distance | | | Standard Deviation | |
Classification	Miles	Kms		Miles	Kms
MCC	10.6	17.1		13.7	22.1
FCC	16.4	26.4		16.8	27.0
PSC	24.3	39.1		18.1	29.1
CSC	31.2	50.2		21.2	34.1
SWR	49.9	80.3		25.0	40.2
PWR	87.5	140.8		52.7	84.8

The entries in Table 19 record the distances rural dwellers travelled to shop in communities at each level in the hierarchy in 1991.

The information provided by the specific shopping patterns, combined with that for distances travelled, assists in interpreting the observations discussed in Chapter 4 on changes to the structure of the system. The substantial decline in functional status of centres below the Secondary Wholesale-Retail level is consistent with present shopping patterns. Only Partial Shopping centres play anything but a trivial role in servicing the needs of communities below themselves in trade-centre status. The ten Wholesale-Retail centres satisfy the requirements for virtually all high-order items for residents of all lower-level communities.

7

Variations from the General Pattern

Introduction

Departures from the general pattern describing changes in the provincial trade-centre system occur under a variety of circumstances. Variations based on differences in the productivity of agriculture in the region served by the community (or communities) were discussed in Chapter 5. Major geographic regions were identified which influenced the evolution of trade centres within areas several thousand square miles in size.

Shopping patterns, too, can effect the structure of the system but between functional categories in this case, moreso than between geographic regions.

At a microlevel other factors, much more local in nature, can influence the fortunes of a single community or a small group of communities.

In this chapter, we consider three types of circumstances which can affect the economy of one or more communities to such an extent that their experience departs from that of other centres in the same functional classification. The three circumstances are: proximity to a much larger centre, the presence of a major mine in the immediate vicinity of the community, and the presence of one or more manufacturing establishments in or near the community.

Proximity to a Major Centre: The Bedroom Effect

When two communities of more or less the same size, and with a similar functional structure, are located relatively close to one another a competitive relationship characterizes their interactions. In a growing economy both communities could expand and possibly develop noncompetitive specializations. In a static or declining context, on the other hand, the competitive struggle often leads to one community emerging as dominant over the other. Much of the "thinning out" of centres in the Full Convenience and Partial

Shopping centre categories between 1961 and 1990 can be attributed to a struggle for local dominance in which one centre retained its status while the other declined one, or even two, functional classifications.

When adjacent communities are very different in size and functional complexity, a complementary relationship is more likely to develop. Bedroom communities represent a specific version of complementarity. As a large community expands, small communities within the immediate vicinity may become residential enclaves of the major centre, though separated geographically. Such small centres may initially have been rural service centres in their own right, but take on a different or additional role as the larger centre grows.

In Saskatchewan most communities initially in the Minimum and Full Convenience categories, situated within thirty-five miles of Saskatoon or Regina, have acquired, to varying degrees, the function of bedroom communities — residential extensions of the two major cities.

The question of how far away from the city a community might be situated and still experience the bedroom effect was approached in three ways. First, bedroom communities are typically domiciles for people who work in the adjacent city. Thus the time required to travel to work has an important bearing on the distance from the job the commuter is prepared to live. Special tabulations from the *1981 Census of Population* were obtained from Statistics Canada which identified commuting-to-work patterns in Saskatchewan. Commuting patterns to the thirty-one largest centres were tabulated and average distances computed. The weighted average commuting distance to these communities, by workers living elsewhere, was thirty-five miles. Second, several visits were made to communities between thirty and fifty miles from Saskatoon and Regina to attempt to obtain a visual impression of whether there were newer residential subdivisions in the communities and how far away from the city this phenomenon could be observed. Finally, statistical comparisons were made between all communities classified as Minimum and Full Convenience centres in 1961 and those within varying distances up to fifty miles from Saskatoon and Regina. The conclusion derived from this three-way approach was that the bedroom phenomenon was generally evident up to thirty-five miles.

We are aware, of course, that there are examples of people commuting much more than thirty-five miles to work. The Statistics Canada data turned up numerous instances of commutes well in excess of fifty miles. What a single individual is willing to do and what many individuals are prepared to do during a period of adjustment, however, does not establish a long-term pattern. In this case, evidence of a bedroom effect was clearly evident to about thirty-five miles. Beyond that, other influences appeared to modify the willingness of people to live in a more distant community and commute to work elsewhere. For example, some people are willing to live in scenic communities such as Indian Head and Fort Qu'Appelle and commute to Regina, a distance of between forty and forty-five miles. At the same time small, otherwise undifferentiated, rural service centres between thirty and forty miles from the major cities may show little or no bedroom development.

In Tables 20 and 21, thirty-year comparisons are made between fifty-nine communities which were classified as Minimum and Full Convenience centres in 1961, situated within thirty-five miles of Regina or Saskatoon, and all other communities occupying these categories at the same date. The entries in these tables represent the differences between the adjacent and distant communities at three points in time.

In Table 20, the entries in the first column indicate that Minimum Convenience centres adjacent to Regina and Saskatoon had an average of twelve more residents than more distant communities in 1961 but had fewer producers, producers' services and consumers' services. In subsequent years adjacent communities gained population relative to distant communities. Further, a deficit in consumers' and producers' services as well as in number of producers in 1961 turned into small surpluses in the following years. No systematic difference is evident in health facilities, high schools, or grain elevators.

Table 20

Residuals* Comparing 1961 Minimum Convenience Bedroom Communities with the Non-Bedroom Communities in Minimum Convenience Category in 1961

Year	1961	1981	1990
Population	**12.16**	**47.53**	**69.62**
Construction	-0.04	0.13	0.34
Manufacturing	0.01	0.20	0.25
Transportation	-0.01	0.05	0.08
All Producers	**-0.04**	**0.38**	**0.68**
Warehousing	0.00	0.00	-0.02
Farm Equipment	-0.04	0.05	0.03
Bulk Fuel	-0.05	0.01	0.15
Wholesale	0.00	0.00	0.15
Building Materials	0.03	-0.01	-0.01
Business Services	0.00	0.00	-0.01
All Producers' Services	**-0.06**	**0.04**	**0.29**
General Store	-0.44	-0.14	0.15
Grocery Store	0.15	-0.01	-0.01
Special Food	0.00	0.01	-0.01
Auto Sales	0.08	0.00	0.06
Gas Station	0.14	-0.04	-0.06
Clothing Store	-0.02	-0.01	-0.01
Furniture Store	0.03	-0.00	-0.02
Home Furnishings	-0.01	0.08	-0.02
Restaurant	-0.15	0.03	0.06
Drug Store	0.00	0.00	0.00
Special Retail	0.06	-0.02	-0.04
Credit Agency	0.00	-0.00	0.08
Hotel	-0.21	0.02	0.12
Laundries	-0.01	-0.00	-0.00
Personal Services	-0.01	0.00	0.00
Auto Repair	0.01	0.15	0.07
Car Wash	0.06	0.04	0.01
Recreation	-0.02	-0.00	-0.01
Banks and Credit Unions	-0.03	0.01	-0.02
All Consumers' Services	**-0.29**	**0.12**	**0.35**
	Presence	Presence	Presence
Doctors	-0.00	0.00	-0.00
Hospitals	0.00	0.00	0.00
Special Care	-0.00	0.00	0.00
High School	0.03	-0.02	0.01
Elevator	0.00	-0.03	0.06

* Means of the bedroom communities minus means of distant communities.

Table 21
Residuals* Comparing 1961 Full Convenience Bedroom Communities with the Non-Bedroom Communities in Full Convenience Category in 1961

Year	1961	1981	1990
Population	**55.55**	**278.61**	**339.37**
Construction	0.40	2.21	1.84
Manufacturing	0.06	0.23	0.35
Transportation	0.03	0.10	0.27
All Producers	0.48	2.54	2.46
Warehousing	0.00	0.00	0.08
Farm Equipment	0.28	0.11	0.41
Bulk Fuel	-0.00	-0.05	-0.03
Wholesale	0.00	0.00	0.14
Building Materials	-0.12	0.42	0.41
Business Services	0.00	0.00	0.20
All Producers' Services	**0.16**	**0.47**	**1.21**
General Store	-0.14	-0.13	0.00
Grocery Store	0.26	0.15	0.19
Special Food	-0.06	0.10	0.11
Auto Sales	0.04	0.04	-0.01
Gas Station	0.53	0.35	0.35
Clothing Store	-0.04	-0.03	0.11
Furniture Store	0.02	0.01	0.06
Home Furnishings	0.03	0.23	0.00
Restaurant	-0.04	0.20	0.58
Drug Store	0.09	0.08	0.12
Special Retail	0.05	0.39	0.21
Credit Agency	-0.01	0.12	0.29
Hotel	-0.08	0.19	-0.03
Laundries	0.00	-0.01	0.00
Personal Services	-0.04	0.00	-0.02
Auto Repair	-0.14	0.29	0.43
Car Wash	-0.25	-0.02	0.03
Recreation	-0.18	-0.01	0.06
Banks and Credit Unions	0.04	0.11	-0.03
All Consumers' Services	**0.09**	**2.07**	**2.44**
	Presence	Presence	Presence
Doctors	0.08	-0.07	0.19
Hospitals	-0.07	-0.04	-0.04
Special Care	0.04	0.11	0.12
High School	0.03	0.30	0.25
Elevator	0.00	-0.02	0.04

* Means of the bedroom communities minus means of distant communities.

The experience of communities classified as Full Convenience centres in 1961 is compared in Table 21. Adjacent communities were initially larger in terms of population, producers, and both types of services. These differences widened substantially in the following years so that by 1990 adjacent communities had on average 340 more inhabitants and six more business outlets. Adjacent centres did marginally better at retaining or acquiring health facilities and high schools as well.

Further comparisons revealed that, while bedroom communities outperformed distant communities which were in the same functional classification in 1961, they developed differently from those distant communities which by 1990 had attained the same population size as the bedroom communities. Specifically, adjacent communities failed to develop commercial structures that were as large or as diversified as distant communities of the same population size. Apparently, proximity to the major cities has retarded the development of commercial functions in adjacent centres while at the same time stimulating their growth in population.

Similar analyses were conducted of Minimum and Full Convenience centres adjacent to the eight Secondary Wholesale-Retail centres. In the latter case there was no evidence of a *systematic* bedroom effect although there are examples of specific communities where some evidence of the bedroom effect is apparent. The commuting data also indicate that approximately 20 percent of the work force in the eight Secondary Wholesale-Retail centres did reside in outlying areas in 1981.

A statistical analysis of the relationship between population and services for adjacent and nonadjacent communities was carried out in order to determine whether or not communities close to Saskatchewan's cities have different population to services ratios than other communities in the same cluster. Since the services a community offers are more likely to be a function of the population of that community than the other way around, regressions were run, using four functional forms, of services on population. The four functional forms tried were services on population, logged services on population, logged services on logged population, and services on logged population. The first functional form, services on population, proved to be the best overall at describing the relation between services and population in Saskatchewan communities.

Regressions were performed on each cluster for the years 1961 and 1990. Dummy variables were used to see if bedroom communities in each cluster had different slopes and intercepts than the cluster as a whole. Services were calculated by adding producer services and consumer services together. Two regressions of services on population were run for each cluster in each year using the Shazam econometrics package. The first regression considered communities around Saskatoon and Regina separately from the communities around the other eight cities. Dummy variables were used to see if the slopes and the intercepts of these subsets of the cluster were different from the slope and the intercept of the cluster as a whole. The second regression considered bedroom communities around the other eight cities. Again dummy variables were used to see if the slope and the intercept of these bedroom communities were different from the slope and the intercept of the cluster as a whole.

1961 Minimum Convenience Cluster

There were 271 communities in the Minimum Convenience category in 1961. Thirty of these communities were within thirty-five miles of either Saskatoon or Regina, and forty-eight were within thirty-five miles of the other eight major cities in Saskatchewan.

The estimated equation of services on population for all Minimum Convenience centres was:

$$S = 2.4001 + .020675 * P.$$
$$(6.12) \quad (6.88)$$

The raw moment R-squared was 0.786 (t-ratios are in parentheses).

For communities within thirty-five miles of Saskatoon and Regina the estimated equation of services on population had a significantly lower intercept and higher slope. Adjusting the coefficients for the values of the dummy coefficients, the estimated equation was:

$$S = -0.5208 + .040094 * P.$$

This indicates that Minimum Convenience centres of under 150 population close to Saskatoon and Regina had fewer services than those more distant with the same population size. The mean population for Minimum Convenience centres in 1961 was 121.

The relationship between population and services for the communities within thirty-five miles of the other eight cities was not significantly different from that for all Minimum Convenience centres. No bedroom effect was systematically observed for the other eight cities.

1990 Minimum Convenience Cluster

There were 419 communities in the Minimum Convenience category in 1990. Forty-four of these communities were within thirty-five miles of Saskatoon and Regina, and seventy-six were within thirty-five miles of the other eight major cities in Saskatchewan.

The estimated equation of services on population for all Minimum Convenience centres in 1990 was:

$$S = -0.16907 + 0.027961 * P.$$
$$(-1.512) \quad (18.18)$$

The raw moment R-squared was 0.6407.

For communities within thirty-five miles of Saskatoon and Regina the estimated equation of services on population had a significantly lower slope. Adjusting the slope coefficient for the value of the dummy coefficients, the equation becomes:

$$S = -0.16907 + 0.01906 * P.$$

This implies that adjacent (bedroom) communities had fewer services at all population levels than those more distant.

Again, the relationship between population and services for the communities adjacent to the other eight cities was not systematically different from that for all Minimum Convenience centres.

1961 Full Convenience Cluster

There were 189 communities in the Full Convenience category in 1961. Twenty-six of these communities were within thirty-five miles of either Saskatoon or Regina, and forty-three were within thirty-five miles of the other eight major centres in Saskatchewan.

The estimated equation of services on population for all Full Convenience centres in 1961 was:

$$S = 6.3146 + 0.027603 * P.$$
$$(9.28) \quad (10.50)$$

The raw moment R-squared was 0.9687.

For communities within thirty-five miles of Saskatoon and Regina, no systematic differences were detected compared with all Full Convenience centres. No bedroom effect could be established. The same was true for the other eight cities.

1990 Full Convenience Cluster

There were 117 communities in the Full Convenience category in 1990. Fifteen of these were within thirty-five miles of either Saskatoon or Regina, and twenty-seven were within thirty-five miles of the other eight major cities in Saskatchewan.

The estimated equation of services on population for all Full Convenience centres in 1990 was:

$$S = 3.1435 + 0.027118 * P.$$
$$(2.78) \quad (10.98)$$

The raw moment R-squared was 0.9178.

For communities within thirty-five miles of Saskatoon and Regina, the estimated equation of services on population had a significantly lower slope. Adjusting the slope coefficient for the value of the dummy coefficient, the equation becomes:

$$S = 3.1435 + 0.013622 * P.$$

Again, the lower slope implies that fewer services were available in nearby communities at all population levels, than in communities more than thirty-five miles from Saskatoon and Regina.

For communities within thirty-five miles of the other eight cities, no systematic differences from all Full Convenience centres could be established in the relationship between population size and number of services.

Mining Communities

Development of a major mine in the vicinity of a community can produce a local boom in housing and commercial development. Several dramatic examples of this phenomenon were apparent in Saskatchewan during and after the 1960s when potash mines were developed at several locations in the central and southeastern parts of the province.

Table 22
Communities Adjacent to Mines

Mining Employment <50		Mining Employment >50	
	SWR	Adjacent to PWR	Non-Adjacent
Ardill	Estevan	Allen	Bienfait
Biggar		Colonsay	Coronach
Cabri		Delisle	Esterhazy
Chaplin		Vanscoy	Lanigan
Claybank			Rocanville
Eastend			
Fox Valley			
Ormiston			
Unity			
Verwood			
Wood Mountain			

In attempting to determine whether the presence of a mine creates a measure of stability for adjacent communities we first identified twenty-one centres in the southern half of the province which had one or more mines in the immediate vicinity. This group was then divided into two groups: those adjacent to mines providing employment for fifty or more workers and those that employed fewer than fifty. Ten communities were in the first group, eleven in the second. In four of the ten instances where local mining employment exceeded fifty, however, the adjacent communities are within thirty-five miles of Saskatoon. In a fifth case, the community is a secondary Wholesale-Retail centre itself (Estevan). Table 22 provides a summary grouping of mining communities.

Five communities were eliminated from further consideration of the impact of mining developments. Allen, Colonsay, Delisle, and Vanscoy were eliminated because they are close enough to Saskatoon to share in the residential spillover of the larger centre. Estevan was also eliminated because it is a Secondary Wholesale-Retail centre and, as such, plays a major role in the provision of trade and services to a large area in the southeastern part of the province. While mining employment is undoubtably beneficial to these communities, we did not think that we could separate its effect from these other influences.

These exclusions left the group of eleven centres near mines employing fewer than fifty workers and the group of five communities, remote from Saskatoon and Regina, near mines employing more than fifty.

The communities in each of these two groups were compared, over the 1961-90 period, with other remote communities initially occupying the same functional classification. In the case of the eleven communities adjacent to mines with fewer than fifty employees, no systematic differences from the comparison group could be detected. This is not a surprising result since the average employment at the mines in question is substantially less than fifty and it is likely that employees are drawn from several local communities or rural areas.

For the remaining five communities situated near mines, employing fifty or more people, a definite positive influence was apparent. In each case, a large amount of employment was created with the development of the mine. In the cases of Coronach, Esterhazy, Lanigan, and Rocanville, which expanded during the 1961-81 period, a substantial increase in population and the development of residential suburbs followed. Public infrastructure was added and some commercial development followed the population increase. Community growth, occasioned by the opening of the mines, did not generate a process of continuous expansion however. These communities did not rise in status in the central-place hierarchy, nor did they become locations which attracted any substantial amount of other rural-based activity. Rather, the pattern following the initial growth was one of stability at approximately the size attained at the time of expansion. The experience of these four

Table 23
Difference Profiles Comparing Remote Mining Communities with Other Remote Communities by Initial Functional Classification*

	FCC Coronach			PSC Lanigan/Rocanville			CSC Esterhazy		
	1961	1981	1990	1961	1981	1990	1961	1981	1990
Population	107	777	728	-158	574	483	-1084	456	353
Producers	-0.52	7.15	1.23	0.65	2.49	0.08	-0.52	-5.55	-3.38
Prod Serv	-0.84	-0.14	2.17	-0.72	-2.90	1.09	-1.21	-7.83	1.45
Con Serv	-0.99	13.53	14.09	-5.27	10.69	4.74	-20.48	-8.90	-18.69

* Coronach has retained its Full Convenience centre status and Lanigan has retained its Partial Shopping centre status. Rocanville declined from Partial Shopping centre to Full Convenience centre between 1961 and 1981 while Esterhazy declined from Complete Shopping centre to Partial Shopping centre between 1981 and 1990.

mining communities, relative to other remote communities of the same initial functional classification, is recorded in Table 23.

Each community clearly recorded substantial gains in population between 1961-81 relative to their reference groups. Relative gains in businesses, while not as uniform as population, were also apparent. A pattern of modest relative decline in population, and mixed gains and losses in business outlets, between 1981 and 1990 definitely left the communities better off in 1990, relative to their reference groups.

Bienfait represents still another perspective on relative location and the influence of mining employment. Coal mining has long been an important employer in the Estevan area. At the time of our initial observation Bienfait was classified in the Partial Shopping centre category. Its population, 842 in 1961, has remained virtually constant at 835 in 1981 and 856 in 1990, somewhat above its reference group throughout the entire period. Its functional classification declined to Full Convenience centre in 1981 and down to Minimum Convenience centre in 1990, however. Because of its location, only seven miles from Estevan, Bienfait was unable to retain any but the very lowest-order commercial activities as shopping patterns were extended during the 1960s and 1970s.

In summary, a substantial amount of mining employment apparently is capable of assisting in stabilizing a community's population, consumers' services and, perhaps, some other types of businesses if the centre in question is remote from a higher-order community in the central-place system. Proximity to a higher-order centre may lead to loss of commercial activities but retention of population if the single observation on Bienfait can be taken as an example.

Manufacturing Communities

Conventional wisdom is that if a community can attract one or more manufacturing plants, its economic fortunes will be enhanced. Our study of the evolution of Saskatchewan's trade centres over a thirty-year period provides an opportunity to test this proposition.

We approached this topic by first eliminating from our data base all mining and bedroom communities. We then excluded for separate analysis the twenty centres in the lower four functional categories which had more than forty manufacturing employees in 1990. The communities remaining in the data set included those in the lower four functional classifications which had up to forty manufacturing employees. This set was then further divided into two groups: those communities which had an above-average number of manufacturing employees within their 1990 functional classifications and those with a below-average number. Finally, to eliminate the differences between the agricultural zones, the above- and below-average groups were divided into northern, southern, and transition zones. Six subsets of communities were thus identified. These were communities in the northern, southern, or transition zone with:

i. above-average manufacturing employment but with fewer than forty employees
ii. below-average manufacturing employment.

A comparison of these communities between 1961 and 1990, holding them in their 1961 classifications, did not identify systematic differences among them which could be associated with the presence or absence of manufacturing activity.

These comparisons were next extended to include the Primary and Secondary Wholesale-Retail centres. For the Secondary Wholesale-Retail category, four centres are in the north: Yorkton, Prince Albert,

Table 24
Difference Profile for Secondary Wholesale-Retail Communities
(Means of the Northern Zone Minus Means of the Southern Zone)

Year	1961	1981	1990
Population	**2121.50**	**4471.75**	**4803.25**
Construction	7.00	51.00	41.00
Manufacturing	2.75	11.25	10.75
Transportation	0.25	19.50	8.50
All producers	**10.00**	**81.75**	**60.25**
Warehousing	2.25	1.50	2.75
Farm equipment	0.50	-4.25	0.50
Bulk fuel	0.50	0.50	1.50
Wholesale	2.75	7.75	5.50
Building materials	2.75	4.50	4.50
Business services	-0.75	8.75	14.50
All producers' serv	**8.00**	**18.75**	**29.25**
General store	0.00	1.50	0.00
Grocery store	10.25	16.00	12.00
Special food	-1.00	5.25	4.50
Auto sales	-2.50	6.00	7.75
Gas station	1.25	7.25	6.50
Clothing store	4.50	7.25	8.00
Furniture store	-1.00	1.75	2.00
Home furnishing	-1.50	8.25	7.00
Restaurant	2.25	16.00	15.50
Drug store	1.50	2.75	2.50
Special retail	-1.75	5.25	19.00
Credit agency	0.00	5.50	33.75
Hotel	2.00	1.75	0.50
Laundries	0.00	-2.25	2.50
Personal services	1.00	1.75	2.50
Auto repair	0.50	4.75	5.00
Car wash	-3.50	8.75	10.50
Recreation	-1.00	2.25	-0.25
Banks and Credit Unions	-0.25	0.50	0.25
All consumers' serv	**10.75**	**100.25**	**139.50**
Doctors	0.00	0.00	0.00
Hospitals	0.00	0.00	0.00
Special care	0.00	0.00	0.00
High school	0.00	0.00	0.00
Elevator	0.00	0.00	0.00

Table 25
Difference Profile for Secondary Wholesale-Retail Communities
(Means of the Northern Zone Minus Means of the Transition Zone)

Year	1961	1981	1990
Population	**-7702.00**	**-4934.75**	**-4961.25**
Construction	-8.00	7.50	14.00
Manufacturing	-9.75	-2.75	0.75
Transportation	-6.25	10.50	11.50
All producers	**-24.00**	**15.25**	**26.25**
Warehousing	0.25	2.00	1.75
Farm equipment	2.50	1.75	4.00
Bulk fuel	0.50	-2.00	-1.00
Wholesale	-6.25	-1.25	7.50
Building materials	-1.75	3.50	0.50
Business services	0.25	7.75	8.00
All producers' serv	**-4.50**	**11.75**	**20.75**
General store	2.00	3.50	-2.00
Grocery store	-10.25	-2.50	2.00
Special food	-10.50	-0.25	2.50
Auto sales	-2.50	3.50	5.75
Gas station	-9.75	1.25	3.00
Clothing store	-4.50	8.75	5.50
Furniture store	0.50	1.75	2.50
Home furnishing	-3.50	2.75	10.00
Restaurant	-7.75	-3.00	7.50
Drug store	-0.50	1.25	1.00
Special retail	-9.75	-3.75	16.00
Credit agency	0.00	4.00	5.75
Hotel	-4.00	-2.25	-4.00
Laundries	0.50	1.25	0.50
Personal services	-0.50	0.25	2.00
Auto repair	-1.50	5.75	9.50
Car wash	-9.00	0.75	5.00
Recreation	-0.50	0.75	-1.25
Banks and Credit Unions	-0.75	0.00	0.25
All consumers' serv	**-72.25**	**23.75**	**71.50**
Doctors	0.00	0.00	0.00
Hospitals	0.00	0.00	0.00
Special care	0.00	0.00	0.00
High school	0.00	0.00	0.00
Elevator	0.00	0.00	0.00

North Battleford, and Lloydminster; two are in the south: Swift Current and Weyburn; and two are in the transition zone: Moose Jaw and Estevan. Difference profiles between the north and the south and between the north and the transition zone are shown in Tables 24 and 25. Referring first to the north-south comparison, northern communities were somewhat larger and had, on average, twenty-nine more business outlets than their southern counterparts in 1961. In the following three decades, the initial advantage of northern communities was magnified many times. Manufacturing as well as other producers, wholesaling and business services increased much more rapidly in northern centres. A rapid growth in number and variety of consumers' services accompanied the expansion of their basic industries. In this instance, relative gains in consumers' services outpaced all other categories of business, reflecting both the growing role of the Secondary Wholesale-Retail level in the trade-centre hierarchy and the loss of population in the southern zone compared with at least modest population growth in the north.

The comparison between northern and transition communities reveals a similar pattern of relative gains for the north. Starting at an initial disadvantage in population and all commercial activity, northern communities had gained a commercial advantage by 1981 which was further strengthened in the following decade. The initial disadvantage in population was reduced from 7,702 in 1961 to 4,961 in 1990.

The final macrocomparison, between Saskatoon and Regina, is shown in Table 26. Once more, the growth of the northern city substantially outpaced its more southerly counterpart (actually Regina is in the transition zone). Beginning with a disadvantage in population and all categories of business functions, Saskatoon's growth subsequently dominated Regina's in all dimensions. Manufacturing and wholesaling registered substantial relative gains and undoubtably contributed to Saskatoon's faster rate of growth. Saskatoon's gains in consumer-service activities were half again as large as its gains in population, percentage-wise, again reflecting the increasing dominance of larger centres in the trade-centre system and the northern region over the southern and transition zones.

Table 26
Difference Profile for Primary Wholesale-Retail Communities (Means of the Northern Zone Minus Means of the Transition Zone)

Year	1961	1981	1990
Population	-16615.00	-8437.00	4087.00
Construction	-33.00	205.00	66.00
Manufacturing	-30.00	71.00	112.00
Transportation	0.00	-17.00	8.00
All producers	**-63.00**	**259.00**	**186.00**
Warehousing	-3.00	-5.00	-20.00
Farm equipment	-6.00	4.00	11.00
Bulk fuel	4.00	0.00	5.00
Wholesale	-44.00	43.00	66.00
Building materials	7.00	38.00	23.00
Business services	-6.00	-32.00	-31.00
All producers' serv	**-48.00**	**48.00**	**54.00**
General store	4.00	-5.00	3.00
Grocery store	-13.00	8.00	-45.00
Special food	-22.00	3.00	9.00
Auto sales	9.00	13.00	-15.00
Gas station	-7.00	17.00	2.00
Clothing store	-2.00	-14.00	64.00
Furniture store	2.00	29.00	22.00
Home furnishing	4.00	6.00	-14.00
Restaurant	14.00	19.00	9.00
Drug store	-2.00	12.00	1.00
Special retail	-20.00	39.00	32.00
Credit agency	0.00	-4.00	192.00
Hotel	4.00	3.00	16.00
Laundries	-1.00	0.00	-2.00
Personal services	-3.00	-6.00	10.00
Auto repair	-7.00	-23.00	4.00
Car wash	-11.00	18.00	39.00
Recreation	0.00	8.00	2.00
Banks and Credit Unions	1.00	0.00	0.00
All consumers' serv	**-50.00**	**123.00**	**329.00**
Doctors	0.00	0.00	0.00
Hospitals	0.00	0.00	0.00
Special care	0.00	0.00	0.00
High school	0.00	0.00	0.00
Elevator	0.00	0.00	1.00

These macrocomparisons do not unequivocally establish that the manufacturing industry was the reason why northern communities outperformed those in the south, of course. As discussed in Chapter 5, the greater diversity of both the agricultural and the nonagricultural base in the north undoubtably facilitated the development of a greater variety of processing and manufacturing than what was possible in the south. Higher population densities in the north also made it easier both to recruit potential employees and produce for local markets. Nevertheless, it is of interest to note that for Primary and Secondary Wholesale-Retail centres, a faster rate of growth in manufacturing activity was part of the process in which northern economic growth exceeded that in the southern and transition zones.

The final comparison involved those twenty communities in the lower four functional categories which had over forty manufacturing employees in 1990. As it turned out, ten of these centres had over 100 manufacturing employees and ten had more than forty but fewer than 100.

Through a lengthy iterative process it became apparent that communities with 100 or more manufacturing employees were larger and more stable through time than those with fewer or no manufacturing employment. The group with over 100 employees in 1990 included eight centres which were in the Complete Shopping centre category in 1961. In this group of eight were the only six communities in the province retaining Complete Shopping centre status throughout the 1961-90 period. Two of those in the initial eight declined one classification to Partial Shopping centre status between 1981 and 1990. Thus three-quarters of the Complete Shopping centres with more than 100 manufacturing employees had retained their status for the past thirty years, while none of the initial Complete Shopping centres with fewer than 100 retained their status. The remaining two communities in the group of ten were Hudson Bay and St. Brieux. Hudson Bay was of the same status in 1990 as 1961 but had risen one classification between 1961 and 1981 and then dropped back to its initial classification between 1981 and 1990. Overharvesting the forest resource upon which Hudson Bay depends has led to the recent contraction of its manufacturing sector. St. Brieux started out as a Full Convenience centre but declined to

Table 27
Communities in the Lower Four Functional Categories*
With More than Forty Manufacturing Employees in 1990

Employment >100	Cluster		
	1961	1981	1990
Hudson Bay	3	4	3
Meadow Lake	4	4	4
Humboldt	4	4	4
Melfort	4	4	4
Tisdale	4	4	4
Biggar	4	4	3
St. Brieux	2	1	1
Wynyard	4	4	3
Nipawin	4	4	4
Kindersley	4	4	4
Employment > 40 <100			
Unity	4	4	3
Watson	3	3	3
Zenon Park	3	2	1
Wadena	4	4	3
Davidson	3	3	3
St. Gregor	2	1	2
Preeceville	3	3	3
Drake	2	1	1
Carlyle	3	3	3
Bruno	3	2	2

*4 = Complete Shopping centre; 3 = Partial Shopping centre; 2 = Full Convenience centre;
1 = Minimum Convenience centre

Minimum Convenience status between 1961 and 1981. In this case, it appears as if the manufacturing activity was initiated after the community had declined within the trade-centre system. As with mining employment, however, reversal of decline in trade-centre status is uncommon. Employment in manufacturing or other economic base-type activity appears capable of stabilizing a community's population but not of altering established shopping patterns — at least not over the range of experiences we have observed. Employment on a truly massive scale would, of course, have a different effect. Communities with more than forty manufacturing employees are shown in Table 27.

The second group of communities, with between forty and 100

Table 28
Difference Profile for Complete Shopping Centres (Communities with Manufacturing Employment >100 - All Other Complete Shopping Centres)

Year	1961	1981	1990
Population	**828.34**	**1439.46**	**1760.20**
Construction	1.87	9.40	7.87
Manufacturing	1.09	4.21	6.04
Transportation	0.54	2.26	3.26
All Producers	**3.50**	**15.87**	**17.17**
Warehousing	0.50	1.30	0.96
Farm Equipment	0.57	1.10	1.49
Bulk Fuel	-0.01	1.49	0.56
Wholesale	1.89	3.33	3.84
Building Materials	-0.11	2.17	2.80
Business Services	0.00	0.70	2.29
All Producers' Serv	**2.83**	**10.09**	**11.93**
General Store	1.63	1.33	1.37
Grocery Store	1.60	3.20	1.11
Special Food	0.39	0.54	1.91
Auto Sales	1.36	2.03	0.31
Gas Station	1.19	2.89	2.73
Clothing Store	0.64	3.09	4.41
Furniture Store	0.26	0.51	0.73
Home Furnishings	0.01	1.23	3.64
Restaurant	0.50	0.54	6.20
Drug Store	0.27	0.71	0.23
Special Retail	0.63	4.87	4.67
Credit Agency	0.00	0.63	6.76
Hotel	0.97	1.16	2.24
Laundries	-0.11	-0.06	0.44
Personal Services	0.37	1.64	1.14
Auto Repair	2.24	1.90	2.16
Car wash	-0.11	2.13	1.89
Recreation	0.39	0.93	1.19
Banks and Credit Unions	0.54	0.86	0.93
All Consumers' Serv	**12.76**	**30.13**	**44.07**
Doctors	0.00	0.00	0.00
Hospitals	0.00	0.00	0.00
Special Care	0.53	0.00	0.00
High School	0.00	0.00	0.00
Elevator	0.00	0.07	0.07

(Grouped on 1961 Cluster, Bedroom and Mining Communities Excluded)

Table 29
Difference Profile for Partial Shopping Centres (Communities with Manufacturing Employment > 40 <100 - All Other Partial Shopping Centres)

Year	1961	1981	1990
Population	**303.08**	**445.07**	**477.11**
Construction	1.05	4.29	3.90
Manufacturing	0.60	4.11	3.47
Transportation	-0.01	1.97	1.14
All Producers	**1.63**	**10.36**	**8.52**
Warehousing	0.00	0.00	0.20
Farm Equipment	0.21	1.35	1.79
Bulk Fuel	-0.07	0.42	0.97
Wholesale	0.00	0.00	0.59
Building Materials	0.92	1.26	0.58
Business Services	0.00	0.00	0.86
All Producers' Serv	**1.07**	**3.03**	**4.99**
General Store	0.87	0.51	0.53
Grocery Store	0.05	0.56	1.48
Special Food	-0.07	0.06	0.35
Auto Sales	0.73	1.30	0.79
Gas Station	0.68	0.92	0.75
Clothing Store	0.19	1.73	1.68
Furniture Store	0.09	0.62	0.26
Home Furnishings	-0.35	0.37	0.71
Restaurant	0.70	0.23	0.88
Drug Store	-0.07	0.21	0.14
Special Retail	-0.05	1.20	2.09
Credit Agency	-0.01	-0.07	0.74
Hotel	0.23	1.37	1.71
Laundries	0.40	0.26	0.24
Personal Services	0.11	-0.06	0.56
Auto Repair	-0.68	0.40	0.67
Car Wash	0.66	0.84	0.67
Recreation	0.24	0.19	0.10
Banks and Credit Unions	-0.07	0.06	0.58
All Consumers' Serv	**3.63**	**10.66**	**14.94**
Doctors	-0.04	-0.05	0.17
Hospitals	-0.07	-0.06	-0.06
Special Care	-0.03	0.33	0.25
High School	-0.04	0.07	0.06
Elevator	0.00	0.01	0.01

(Grouped on 1961 Cluster, Bedroom and Mining Communities Excluded)

manufacturing employees, was then investigated. This group included two communities initially classified as Complete Shopping centres which subsequently declined to Partial Shopping centre status. Six communities, initially in the Partial Shopping centre category were also included. Four of these six centres (67 percent) retained their status through the past thirty years compared with only 17 percent of the other communities classified as Partial Shopping centres in 1961 which were still in this category in 1990. Two other communities, initially Full Convenience centres, round out the group. One (St. Gregor) was in the same category in 1990 as in 1961, while a second (Drake) had declined to Minimum Convenience status between 1961 and 1981.

In Table 28 the eight communities classified as Complete Shopping centres in 1961, which had over 100 manufacturing employees in 1990, are compared with the other twenty-one communities in the province which were of the same status in 1961. Starting from an initial advantage in population and all commercial groupings, these eight thoroughly outperformed their counterparts over the three decades. Relative gains in consumers' services, while substantial, did not keep pace with relative gains in producers or producers' services, indicating that these communities have become the dominant trading centre in their area but play a limited role in the expanded regional trade-centre context as identified in the chapter on shopping patterns.

In Table 29 a similar comparison is made of the six communities which were of Partial Shopping centre status in 1961, and had between forty and 100 manufacturing employees in 1990, and the other ninety-three centres which were in the same classification in 1961. The results are similar to the previous comparison, though on a smaller scale. The initial advantage in population and commercial services increased through time, although their manufacturing advantage slipped somewhat between 1981 and 1990. Again the relative gain in consumers' services, while impressive, is not as great as in other commercial categories. In this comparison, an initial disadvantage in infrastructure is largely eliminated over the three decades.

In deriving some tentative conclusions on the effect of manufacturing activity it is necessary to keep several considerations in mind. The first is the north-south distinction. Northern communities outperformed southern communities in virtually every comparison. Most of the communities identified in Table 27 are in the northern zone. Within this zone, most Complete Shopping centres which had more than 100 manufacturing employees retained their status and grew faster than those with fewer than 100. But a chicken-and-egg question arises. Were these communities already sufficiently attractive because of location on the transportation network, or did the local commercial outlets have a sufficiently good reputation that they were emerging as locally dominant communities which then drew the manufacturing firms to their already viable location? Or was it the growth of the manufacturing activity which added population and strengthened the other commercial sectors? It is not possible to know with certainty.

Nevertheless, the presence of manufacturing activity of locally substantial proportions is associated with above-average retention of trade-centre status and performance considerably better than communities with fewer manufacturing jobs.

Giving the benefit of the doubt, perhaps it can be concluded from this that 100 or more manufacturing jobs can assist in stabilizing a community which is well situated on the regional transportation network and which has a sufficient complement of trade and service outlets for it to play a locally important role in the trade-centre system. The experience of St. Brieux on the other hand, which is poorly situated and whose trade-centre status had declined before the manufacturing presence expanded to its present size, illustrates that even a relatively large manufacturing development is unlikely to reverse past decline in trade-centre status.

Employment of between forty and 100 also appears to contribute to stability, but at a lower level. Thus there is no example of a Complete Shopping centre, with employment within this range, which retained its status. Partial Shopping centres, however, with employment in this range, did retain their status at a higher rate than those with fewer manufacturing employees.

The number of communities in Table 27 is obviously too small to permit strong conclusions but, to the extent that it is possible to derive a message from these data, it might be as follows: substantial manufacturing employment can contribute to the stability and perhaps even enhance the trade-centre status of a community that is favourably situated and presently viable within the trade-centre network. For communities that are poorly situated or have already declined to Full or Minimum Convenience status, manufacturing employment may lead to results similar to those observed in the section on mining. That is, even substantial employment may do no more than stabilize the population. It is unlikely to reverse or even sustain the trade-centre role once it has fallen below a critical level.

8

Public and Private Investment

Background

A community consists of more than just a group of private households and private businesses. Publicly provided streets and sidewalks, sewer and water systems, street lights and cemeteries are part of the physical environment of nearly all communities. In addition, local and provincial governments have a presence in nearly every centre. In larger communities there may even be a federal government presence.

The employees who work for the various levels of government are typically situated in structures owned or leased by their employers. Some buildings are simply offices which could lend themselves to a variety of alternative private or public uses. Often, however, the structures themselves are specialized according to function. Thus hospitals, schools, libraries, and fire halls are examples of structures designed for a particular use and generally are of limited usefulness in activities other than those for which they were designed. These specialized structures, created to assist in the delivery of a specific set of goods or services, are publically owned in most cases.

Government services, provided at the community level, are distributed in rough proportion to the population served although, as with commercial functions, there is something like a demand threshold that dictates the spatial distribution of each particular function. Thus elementary schools, like gasoline stations, are found in even very small communities. Hospitals, on the other hand, like higher-order commercial functions, are found in fewer and larger places.

In communities that are growing, investment in public infrastructure is an ongoing activity both to create new capacity and to upgrade existing structures. Such activity provides employment during the construction phase, creates employment when it is put to use, and in the case of infrastructure designed to serve the population of a region, becomes a focal point for people from smaller communities and rural areas as well as those from the centre in which it is situated. The infrastructure itself then adds to the attraction of a community, complementing and reinforcing the array of goods and services provided by the commercial sector.

In a stable or declining centre, the major impetus to infrastructure creation — population growth — is absent. Even upgrading is approached with greater caution. In a growing community, upgrading may postpone more expensive new construction. In a slow or no-growth situation, the question is implicitly or explicitly raised as to whether future utilization will justify the improvement in quality made possible by upgrading. The more specialized the infrastructure, the greater is this risk. Thus in the absence of pressure on capacity, existing facilities continue to be utilized and the greater the local contribution, the more cautious is the approach to a commitment. Through time, the infrastructure in declining and even stable communities becomes increasingly inferior to that in growing centres. The differences in infrastructure reinforce widening differences in commercial offerings available in communities that are becoming larger compared with those that are not.

Analysis of Expenditures on Infrastructure

To examine the recent pattern of infrastructure creation, actual (and planned) investment expenditures in Saskatchewan communities by the provincial government and the Saskatchewan Wheat Pool (SWP) were obtained for the period 1981/82-1990/91. These records indicate that the provincial government made expenditures on, or contributions toward, a variety of public facilities: court houses, rural service centres, weigh scales, health centres, hospitals, schools of several types, town halls, low-income housing, and a variety of office buildings. The SWP's expenditures were, of course, related to its grain-handling and storage activity and were focussed on its once ubiquitous grain elevators.

A summary of the results of this analysis is presented in Table 30. There were 464 communities in which expenditures were recorded. The total population of communities in which expenditures were

Table 30
Population and Provincial Government Plus SWP Investment:
1981-1991

		Nominal Dollars			
Functional Classification	Total Population	Total Expenditure ($)	Average Population	Average Expenditure ($)	Expenditure/ Population ($)
MCC	51,937	25,775,966.75	181	89,811.73	496.29
FCC	66,645	123,723,745.04	578	1,075,858.65	1,861.49
PSC	80,901	127,929,241.98	1,759	2,781,070.48	1,581.31
CSC	29,234	94,362,105.85	4,872	15,727,017.64	3,227.82
SWR	144,706	223,482,926.55	18,088	27,935,365.82	1,544.39
PWR	362,887	1,800,828,299.12	181,434	900,414,149.56	4,962.50

made are recorded in the second column opposite the 1990 functional classification of the community group.

Total expenditures over the decade by functional classification are found in the third column from the left. These totals sum to 2.4 billion nominal dollars. They exclude expenditures in the north (Census Division 18) and expenditures where a location could not be determined, as well as expenditures on intercity highways and those made in a completely rural setting. The expenditures recorded in the table refer only to those which could be identified as made in, or immediately adjacent to, a community.

The average population column refers to the average population of those communities in which expenditures were actually made — not the average population of centres in that functional classification. Thus the population figure of 181 for Minimum Convenience centres is well above the average size for this category (141) indicating that, on average, expenditures were made in communities that were above-average size in this classification. No expenditures were made in many of the smallest Minimum Convenience centres. Some expenditures were made in most communities above the Minimum Convenience category.

Average expenditure refers to the average investment outlay per community in which expenditures were made. For all but the Minimum Convenience category these numbers are close to the averages per community in the classification since some expenditures

Table 31
Cumulative Expenditures on Community Infrastructure
by Functional Classification

Functional Classification	Cumulative %	Cumulative # of Centres
Primary Wholesale-Retail	75.16	2
Secondary Wholesale-Retail	84.48	10
Complete Shopping Centre	88.42	16
Partial Shopping Centre	93.76	62
Full Convenience Centre	98.92	179
Minimum Convenience Centre	100.00	464

were made in nearly every community. For Minimum Convenience centres, the $89,811 refers to the average for those communities in which some investment actually occurred.

The final column identifies the expenditures per capita in communities where investments were made.

Overall, community-based investment expenditures approximate the population distribution of Saskatchewan's trade-centre system. Comparing either total population and total expenditure or average population and average expenditure reveals close correspondence between population and infrastructure investment.[1]

On a per capita basis, expenditures were lowest in Minimum Convenience centres and highest in Complete Shopping and Primary Wholesale-Retail centres. What has to be recognized, of course, is that an expenditure of $28 million in a Secondary Wholesale-Retail centre, the category with the second lowest per capita allocation, will create a much greater *concentration* of infrastructure (and therefore attraction) than $1 million spent in a Full Convenience centre even though the per capita expenditure in the latter is 20 percent higher than in the former.

An impression of the concentrating effect of infrastructure investment is provided in Table 31 by arranging the data to focus on cumulative expenditures. Saskatoon and Regina received 75 percent of combined provincial and SWP infrastructure investment during the decade of the 1980s. The ten cities accounted for 84 percent, the sixteen largest places 88 percent, and so on. To point out this distribution is not to criticize the concentration in the few largest communities. The major concentration of the population is in the cities. Further, some infrastructure, such as the base hospitals in Saskatoon and Regina, for example, serve the entire provincial population as verified by the shopping patterns recorded in Chapter 6.

For some public services something much like economies of scale characterize their operations. In addition, they rely on sophisticated urban service-support systems and a central location on air and highway transportation networks. Consequently, it is unlikely that high-order public services could function as efficiently from other than a large facility in a central location.

Nevertheless, this spatial pattern of infrastructure expenditure reinforces centralizing influences associated with changing production, communications and distribution technology and with the increasingly urban-oriented shopping preferences of rural dwellers.

Investment in Commercial Infrastructure

Cooperatively organized retail outlets are found in many communities in Saskatchewan at each level in the trade-centre system.

It was anticipated that investment expenditures made by cooperative organizations could reflect the pattern of private-sector capacity creation and upkeep.

Federated Co-ops provided information on investment expenditures. Unfortunately, however, investment data was available in accessible form for only 1985 through 1990. This proved to be too short a period to identify the long-term investment strategy of the cooperative system. Substantial investment had taken place in the preceding years; much less investment had occurred during the relatively depressed second half of the 1980s.

Investment data were replaced with gross sales data which were available for the entire decade. A close correspondence between population distribution and gross sales was observed over the entire trade-centre hierarchy. Population distribution "explained" three-quarters of the spatial distribution of sales within the network of retail cooperatives. An alternative formulation was then tried focussing on only the communities in the lower four functional classifications. At this level, population distribution "explained" 80 percent of the spatial distribution of sales and appears to lend credence to the impression that retail cooperatives are somewhat more concentrated in the province's smaller communities.[2]

Although the sales data are generally consistent with the pattern of infrastructure investment, sales convey information on existing expenditure patterns whereas investment is more likely to reflect an anticipation of future patterns.

NOTES

1. The results for the analysis of total population and total expenditure produced a correlation coefficient of 0.96998 and a Spearman rank correlation coefficient of 0.94286.

   The results for the analysis of average population and average expenditure were a correlation coefficient of 0.99788 and a Spearman rank correlation coefficient of 1.00000.

2. Over the six clusters, the correlation between total population and total gross sales was 0.72648. The Spearman rank correlation coefficient was 0.77951. A second test was then made using total gross sales and total population in the lower four clusters. The correlations were somewhat higher, 0.80971 for the correlation coefficient and 0.80949 for the rank correlation coefficient.

9

Options for the Future

The private and public infrastructure presently in place in rural Saskatchewan reflects a settlement pattern developed in the context of historical technologies. Through time, improved technology has made much of the capacity in rural commercial enterprises and rural public infrastructure redundant. Preferences of rural dwellers for variety, quality, and lower prices, available only in larger centres, has further reduced the use of much private and public capacity. In response to these influences, the trade-centre system has been in a process of consolidation for several decades.

Provincial and federal government infrastructure investment has responded to the requirements of an increasingly urban population. In the rural context, however, both levels of government have attempted, at least from the 1960s, to slow if not prevent the consolidation that inevitably followed adoption of new technologies. That these attempts have failed is evident by the existence of a substantial overcapacity of both public and private infrastructure, much of which is of an inferior technology and nearing the end of even its physical life. Seldom used branch lines and (some) grid roads, unoccupied hospital beds and underutilized schools, empty serviced lots and unoccupied industrial parks, "for sale" signs on a very substantial portion of private houses in small communities, buildings downgraded from a previously higher order to a new lower-order use, vacant commercial space and boarded-up stores provide visual evidence that the system is consolidating. In spite of this, governments have failed to revise their rural presence in a way that is consistent with the inevitable adjustment. Even those people who continue to live in rural Saskatchewan hasten the process of consolidation through the use of commercial, recreational, medical, and other facilities in distant urban centres while underutilized capacity exists closer to their homes.

Important decisions must soon be made. Because of the magnitude of public expenditures, and their mandates to lead, governments will have a major influence in defining the environment within which the trade-centre system evolves over the next many years.

Conceptually, the options lie on a continuum, the midpoint of which is a "do nothing" approach in which the rural economy is essentially left to fend for itself. Movement away from the midpoint in either direction involves increasingly focussed intervention. What distinguishes one direction from the other is the vision of the future for rural Saskatchewan. In one direction, government activities would be directed by a recognition and accommodation of changing technologies and the demonstrated preferences of rural dwellers; in the opposite, actions would be guided by a commitment to oppose the changes which follow the introduction of new technologies and evolving preferences.

With either approach the functional and spatial consequences of infrastructure investment would have to be accommodated to ensure consistency with the objectives. In the past this reconciliation has not been part of the planning process. Provincial and federal governments have taken advantage of emerging technologies in an effort to provide services in a cost-effective manner. The same governments selectively attempted to oppose the negative effects that inevitably followed by retaining unused or seldom-used facilities or distributing infrastructure investment so that expenditures were made in as many communities as possible. This approach has undoubtably accelerated consolidation through diverting funds that could have been better used elsewhere to the maintenance of unproductive capacity and by dissipating the attraction that could occur if a complete complement of infrastructure was grouped in selected locations.

With unlimited resources governments could create capacity and employment in enough rural communities to dramatically slow or possibly prevent further consolidation. The size of accumulated provincial and federal debt eliminates this technically possible alternative as a realistic option however. Nevertheless, substantial expenditures will continue to be made for upkeep and replacement of public facilities in rural Saskatchewan. How and where these expenditures are made will have a major influence on the structure of the trade-centre system of the future. Private corporations and cooperatives with geographically widespread facilities have the potential to participate in a coherent vision of rural Saskatchewan as well through their own reorganizations, consolidations, and investment in new facilities.

Perhaps the time has come to choose a feasible vision for rural Saskatchewan. Concerted and deliberate intervention designed to oppose the effects of new technology and evolving preferences would be very expensive but would likely slow the pace of consolidation. The pursuit of cost-minimizing efficiency would be less expensive but would further contribute to consolidation.

The most intriguing question may be whether there is an approach which would coordinate decisions among government departments and private companies that would preserve as many viable rural communities as possible without incurring too great a sacrifice in terms of efficiency. Such an approach would recognize the emergence of a group of strong rural centres and would build upon their strengths. These are the logical sites for the concentration of rural infrastructure. It has been demonstrated as well that rural manufacturing activity can make an important contribution to the viability of rural communities that are well located on the transport network and are still playing a locally important role in the trade centre context. Future research could inquire further into why manufacturers select a particular community and how rural communities could encourage manufacturers to locate in their centre. The development of entrepreneurship is another important topic for further research. The fact that only a modest number of individuals — a few hundred out of a population of a million — have taken the initiative and risk to develop a rural manufacturing establishment may imply that the risks are unduly high or that there is a lack of entrepreneurial orientation that could be addressed through some type of public initiative.

Then, of course, there is the possibility of choosing to continue with the unfocussed practices of past decades or to retain this approach through default by failing to deliberately chart a new course. This alternative would lead to further substantial consolidation without realizing the efficiencies of the cost-minimizing alternative.

References

Anding, Thomas L. et al. 1990. *Trade Centers of the Upper Midwest: Changes From 1960 to 1989*. Minneapolis, MN: Center for Urban and Regional Affairs, University of Minnesota.

Bangsund, Dean. A., F. Larry Leistritz, Janet K. Wanzek, Dale Zetocha and Holly E. Bastow-Shoop. 1991. *North Dakota Trade Areas: An Overview*. Fargo, ND: North Dakota State University.

Barkley, Andrew P. 1990. "The Determinants of the Migration of Labor Out of Agriculture in the U.S., 1940-85." *American Journal of Agricultural Economics* 72: 567-73.

Barnard, J.R., J.A. MacMillan and W.R. Maki. 1969. "Evaluation Models for Regional Development Planning." *Papers, Regional Science Association* 23: 117-38.

Berry, Brian J.L. et al. 1988. *Market Centers and Retail Location: Theory and Applications*. Englewood Cliffs: Prentice-Hall.

Bollman, Ray. 1990. "Rural and Small Town Canada: An Overview." Paper presented at the Rural and Small Town Canada: Economic and Social Reality Conference, Ottawa.

Borchert, John R. and Russell B. Adams. 1963. *Trade Centers and Tributary Areas of the Upper Midwest*. Minneapolis, MN: University of Minnesota. Upper Midwest Economic Study.

Brown, David L. et al. 1988. *Rural Economic Development in the 1980s: Prospects for the Future*. New York: U.S. Department of Agriculture, Economic Research Service.

Carlino, Gerald and Edwin Mills. 1987. "The Determinants of County Growth." *Journal of Regional Science* 27: 39-54.

Edwards, Clark. 1976. "The Political Economy of Rural Development: Theoretical Perspectives." *American Journal of Agricultural Economics* 58: 914-21.

Flora, Cornelia B. and James A. Christenson, eds. 1991. *Rural Policies for the 1990s*. Boulder, CO: Westview Press.

Furtan, W.H. and G.E. Lee. 1977. "Economic Development of the Saskatchewan Wheat Economy." *Canadian Journal of Agricultural Economics* 25: 15-28.

Hathaway, Dale E. 1960. "Migration from Agriculture: The Historical Record and Its Meaning." *American Economic Review* 50: 379-91.

Hodge, Gerald. 1965. "The Prediction of Trade Centre Viability in the Great Plains." *Papers, Regional Science Association* 15: 87-115.

Jansma, J. Dean and Frank M. Goode. 1976. "Rural Development Research: Conceptualizing and Measuring Key Concepts." *American Journal of Agricultural Economics* 58: 922-27.

John, Dewitt, Sandra Batie, and Kim Norris. 1988. *A Brighter Future for Rural America*. Washington, DC: National Governors' Association.

Levine, D.S. and I. Adelman. 1973. "Economic Development in Appalachia." *Annals of Regional Science* 7: 13-26.

Luloff, A.E. and Louis E. Swanson. 1990. *American Rural Communities*. Boulder, CO: Westview Press.

Mulligan, Gordon F. 1984. "Agglomeration and Central Place Theory: A Review of the Literature." *International Regional Science Review* 9: 1-42.

Nevin, Edward. 1966. "The Case for Regional Policy." *The Three Banks Review* (December): 30-46.

Nuckton, C.F., R.I. Rochin, and D. Gwynn. 1982. "Farm Size and Rural Community Welfare: An Interdisciplinary Approach." *Rural Sociology* 47: 32-46.

Pigg, Kenneth E., ed. 1991. *The Future of Rural America: Anticipating Policies for Constructive Change*. Boulder, CO: Westview Press.

Redman, Barbara. 1980. "Rural Development: A Critique." *American Journal of Agricultural Economics* 62: 1031-36.

Reed, David A. 1989. *The Winnowing: Economic Change in Rural America*. New York: The Hudson Institute.

Saskatchewan. 1957. Royal Commission on Agriculture and Rural Life. *Service Centres*. Regina: Queen's Printer.

Stabler, Jack C. 1986. "Branch Line Abandonment and Prairie Towns: One More Time." *Canadian Journal of Regional Science* 9: 207-19.

Stabler, Jack C. 1987a. "Trade Center Evolution in the Great Plains." *Journal of Regional Science* 27: 225-44.

Stabler, Jack C. 1987b. "Non-Metropolitan Population Growth and the Evolution of Rural Service Centres in the Canadian Prairie Region." *Regional Studies* 21: 43-53.

Stabler, Jack C. and Eric C. Howe. 1988. "Service Exports and Regional Growth in the Postindustrial Era." *Journal of Regional Science* 28: 303-15.

Stabler, Jack C. and Peter R. Williams. 1973. *The Dynamics of a System of Central Places*. Reading, U.K.: University of Reading.

Stabler, Jack C., M.R. Olfert and Murray Fulton. 1992. *The Changing Role of Rural Communities in an Urbanizing World: Saskatchewan 1961-1990*. Regina: Canadian Plains Research Center.

Swanson, Louis E., ed. 1988. *Agriculture and Community Change in the U.S.: The Congressional Research Reports*. Boulder, CO: Westview Press.

United States Department of Agriculture. Economic Research Service. *Rural Conditions and Trends*. Various Issues, 1990-1991.

United States Department of Agriculture. Economic Research Service. *Rural Development Perspectives*. Various Issues, 1985-1991.

75051

DATE DUE

NOV 0 6 2000			
DEC 0 6 2000			
	261-2500		Printed in USA